CHRISTMAS JEV

by Mary M

Revised 3rd Edition

4880 Lower Valley Road, Atglen, Pennsylvania 19310

photographs by James Morrison

Dedication

This book is affectionately dedicated to my sister Nancy Stewart. Her generosity has enriched so many lives.

Revised 3rd Edition

Library of Congress Control Number: 2009929645

Designed by Bonnie M. Hensley
Typeset in Benguiat BK BT/Korinna BT

ISBN: 978-0-7643-3365-1
Printed in China
1 2 3 4 C

Schiffer Books are available at special discounts for bulk purchases for sales promotions or premiums. Special editions, including personalized covers, corporate imprints, and excerpts can be created in large quantities for special needs. For more information contact the publisher:

Published by Schiffer Publishing Ltd.
4880 Lower Valley Road
Atglen, PA 19310
Phone: (610) 593-1777;
Fax: (610) 593-2002
E-mail: Info@schifferbooks.com

For the largest selection of fine reference books on this and related subjects, please visit our web site at **www.schifferbooks.com** We are always looking for people to write books on new and related subjects. If you have an idea for a book please contact us at the above address. This book may be purchased from the publisher. Include $5.00 for shipping. Please try your bookstore first. You may write for a free catalog.

In Europe, Schiffer books are distributed by
Bushwood Books
6 Marksbury Ave.
Kew Gardens
Surrey TW9 4JF England
Phone: 44 (0) 20 8392-8585;
Fax: 44 (0) 20 8392-9876
E-mail: info@bushwoodbooks.co.uk
Website: **www.bushwoodbooks.co.uk**

Acknowledgments

I was fortunate in finding so many willing collectors and dealers who mailed or brought their Christmas jewelry for me to photograph. I am sure that you, as a reader, will appreciate them as I do. In addition to my own, the pieces in this book came from the following collections:

Muriel Allen
Barbara Allenbaugh
Laurel Bailey
Dorothy Bauer
East of Oz/Marie and Michael Dick
Sally Grant
Lee Herling
Shirley Levitt
Marie M. Myers
Ann Mitchell Pittman
Colleen B. Renner
Barbara Runge
Barbara Singer

For help and support I would like to acknowledge:

Laurel Bailey, who answered questions and served as my Christmas pin guide through the maze of manufacturers.

Isabelle Bryman, who founded and owns *jewelcollect*, the online mailing list for costume jewelry collectors. She has urged me on and patiently and efficiently responded to my questions.

The jewelry guy, Paul DeFruscio, whose careful answers to my questions about the most intricate processes of jewelry manufacture were there almost as soon as I asked them.

Jill Gallina, who early on encouraged me to write about Christmas jewelry and offered her help.

Janet Lawwill for the authorized use of a few of the wonderful ideas she has collected and posted on her websitefor costume jewelry care.

To the readers of *jewelcollect*—you know who you are —who took the time to respond to questions, look at pictures and offer encouraging words. Thank you, Deb, Pat, Davida, Ann, and many others.

I am sure every reader is grateful for the beautiful images so carefully photographed by my husband, James Morrison. In some instances, he reshot pieces over and over to get just the effect he hoped for. Without this careful attention to detail, this wonderful Christmas jewelry would not be shown to best advantage; without his participation and encouragement, I would not have begun this project.

Contents

Introduction

How many ways can a Christmas tree be shaped in jewelry? There seems to be no limit. Each year the number of lovely, absolutely fresh designs that appear in stores is astonishing. In addition, shoppers can find variations on old designs. Avid collectors hunt for these pieces in department stores, specialty gift shops, and jewelry stores, knowing that once they have been sold, they may be very difficult to find again. The retail Christmas season may seem unreasonably long for many, but for a collector who is shopping for Christmas jewelry, it seems unreasonably short.

When pins have disappeared from the retail shelves, they go into collections or are tucked away in a reseller's stock. The prices begin to rise, depending on the rarity and desirability of the piece. Now that buying and selling jewelry on the internet has become popular, it is possible to sit at home and see yesterday's after-Christmas, half-priced bargain selling at twice or three times the original price.

Although far more collectors are interested in Christmas trees, there are also snowman seekers, ornament enthusiasts, holly hounds, and those of us who like all Christmas jewelry. One nice thing about collecting Christmas jewelry is that a collector can start on just about any budget. New pins that may become tomorrow's treasures are issued each Christmas from under $10 to several hundred dollars.

The design and manufacture of Christmas rhinestone jewelry started sometime in the late 1940s. An employee of Weiss remembers that a Christmas tree was their biggest selling item one year not long after the end of World War II. Before then, a Christmas corsage decorated a lady's coat or dress during the holiday season. Made of cloth leaves, fabric ribbon, artificial berries, tiny plastic bells, and just about anything else light weight, these fragile decorations would last the season but would probably need to be replaced the next Christmas.

The practice of wearing Christmas corsages may have started even before World War II. Collectors old enough to remember tell me they wore them during the war and perhaps before. The Christmas corsage lasted into the early sixties, then gave way entirely to the metal frame Christmas jewelry we know today.

Christmas jewelry collectors who wear their prizes all year round risk disparaging remarks, even laughter. This does not discourage us. We know what we like.

About the captions

The prices in this book are for pieces in very good to excellent condition, regardless of the condition of the piece pictured. These prices are not intended to set market value, instead they are a reflection of real prices paid in the United States.

I have used some terms that are not common jewelry terms. They are:

layers—this describes the number of pieces of metal riveted together to make a piece (usually a tree). You can determine the number of layers by turning the pin so you can see the edge between the front and the back.

tiers—this tells the number of sections of branches down the side of the tree, looking at the piece from the front.

dimensions—when measuring pieces, I have used the height for trees, but the longest dimension for other pieces that might not necessarily be worn at any specific angle.

The recession beginning in 2008 has triggered an upheaval in the Christmas jewelry market, just as it has in other markets. To some extent, the prices of older, rarer pins have declined, causing many individuals and dealers to hold back until the recession ends. That means that there is simply less in the way of high-end jewelry offered for sale. As a result, some older pins continue to fetch high prices. On the other hand, newer trees and other designs are offered at prices even lower than before; many do not sell at all. Christmas trees continue to be by far the most popular design, with relatively greater decline in values of vintage Christmas boughs, sleighs, little animals, and many others.

Mary Morrison
April, 2009

Four corsages, probably from the forties. You can pick out a chenille snowman, a plastic bell, a celluloid deer, foil candy canes, and tiny brush trees. The earliest of these is probably the fourth; its small beads threaded on chenille were common during, and even before, World War II. 4-5"each. $5-10 each

If you wear your Christmas jewelry only during the holidays, you may find there aren't enough occasions to do your collection justice. Here is one solution. This blazer easily displays eleven pins. With many more than that, it begins to droop and you will begin to tire!

Four miscellaneous signed trees. **a.** Tara jewelry was first made in the 1940s to celebrate the release of the film *Gone with the Wind*. This is a six-tier tree, partly painted green, with five loose garlands. It is decorated with clear, red, and green stones. 2.25" **b.** The *JA* signature on this sterling silver tree stands for J Avery. The lion and lamb, the dove, and the Latin word for "peace" seem to date it to the 1960s. There are no rhinestones on the piece. 1.62" **c.** Signed *Jeanne* on the back, this outline tree is made of ropey metal and bears some similarity to the Napier tree Fig 1.126b. It is decorated with seventeen red and green rhinestones. 2.37" **d.** I have seen this unusual pin, signed *Gold Crown Inc*, in several collections in both gold and silver finish. In this example, the large stones are cabochons. There are three additional stones and a yellow stone in the star at the top. 2.75" See another example in Fig 1.54. $25-60 each

Sometimes Christmas trees will fit nicely into other holiday displays. Here they are, pinned to a Styrofoam mountain that serves as a backdrop for my collection of antique bisque Santas.

This wicker frame Christmas tree is a homemade piece that a friend found in an antique store, covered with Christmas pins. I've used it here to show my own collection of ornament pins, but it could as well display trees or an assortment of Christmas pins.

Opposite page: When this Christmas fabric was offered by the yard in December of 1997, I saw its potential for a pin display.

Chapter 1

Signed Christmas Trees

Alpha. English firm making costume jewelry since 1972. Still in operation. I know of only one Christmas tree.

Fig 1.1 This beautifully crafted tree was made in England by Alpha, but the only evidence is on its paper ticket. This one has the number *98* in an oval on the back, indicating its place in an edition limited to 500. This same tree was made with jelly-like stones of several different colors; this one is ruby. Embedded in the metal framework are tiny clear rhinestones. 1.5" $95-120

ART. ART designed pieces that it contracted for manufacture with jobbers. According to some, this is a completely separate division of Capri. ART was their designer division. 1950-1970s.

Fig 1.2 Three trees signed *ART*. **a.** By far the most elaborate and the loveliest ART tree I have seen, it is constructed with two layers of swooping branches, each branch covered with a row of tiny, clear rhinestones graduated in size. Multicolored rhinestones hang above them as ornaments. The overall effect is spectacular. 2.25" $40-90 **b.** More common two-layer ART tree, here with enameled candles. Only the flames are rhinestones. 1.87" $25-45 **c.** This tree uses a darker brass metal, highlighted with white enameled snow. The candles are also enameled; only the tiny flames are rhinestone. 2.25" $10-35

Fig 1.3 Five trees, all enameled shades of green. These ART trees have been so heavily enameled that they look almost like plastic on the front. They are seldom found with the enamel chipped. **a.** Slightly rounded tree on a dark-colored mound. You can barely peer between its snowy branches. 2.25" **b**. A much darker, three-tiered tree on a large mound with scattered ornaments. 2.12" **c**. Notice the zigzag design on the pot, a design you will see on the containers of other ART trees. The branches are touched with snow, and here again you can see between them to the back. This piece is extravagant in its use of colored rhinestone ornaments—twenty-nine in all, including the star top. It was also offered without the green enamel. 2.25" **d**. This tree is made in two layers, with ornaments attached to branches on each. Here you see what are probably the most characteristic stone colors used on ART Christmas jewelry: orange, bright blue, and amber. 2.12" **e**. You can also see between the branches to the back of this tree. The colored rhinestones in its base are unusual for ART. 2.12" $25-45 each.

Fig 1.4 a. This is probably the easiest ART tree to find. Its branches look like long, thin, drooping deciduous leaves. It is dotted with ornaments of equal size. The base has a trunk with roots that are curved, as if they were freshly dug—another characteristic of some ART trees. 2.37" **b.** Tree made of two layers of snow-dusted branches that swoop forward to give it even more depth. The base of the trunk has roots. 2.25" **c.** The stones here are all on the garlands, which wrap the tree, even slipping under some of its drooping branches. Sometimes this has been called "The ART Garland Tree." 2.25" $15-50 each.

Fig 1.5 Three trees, all with baguette candles by ART. **a.** This is a two-layer tree with tiny, thin candles of various colors. The geometric frame, a solid outline with spider webbing inside, is particularly pretty. 2.12" **b.** Solid tree with five tiers. All the candles are clear, but the rhinestone flames vary in color. The plain, straight trunk is uncommon on ART trees. 2.5" **c.** Two layers of prickly looking branches; tiny clear candles without separate flames dot the front layer. This tree has none of the orange rhinestones that characterize most ART trees. Instead, it has opaque, round, red stones as well as other colors. 2.25" $15-50 each.

Fig 1.6 Three modernistic trees by ART. **a.** Two layers, very open and angular, with ornaments in typical ART colors. 2.25" **b.** Molded in two pieces of different textured metal; a similar tree can be found unsigned. See Fig 4.3a for a matching candle. 2.37" **c.** Another unusual design, this tree is sometimes found in gold. Here, with a light green wash, the stones lie in openings in the tree. 2.12" $20-45 each.

Fig 1.7 a. This tree is uncharacteristic of ART, other than the color of the stones. It is completely flat, has slightly raised edges and stone settings, and is filled with colored enamel. 2.12" **b.** A two-layer tree, this one looks as if they took the one in Fig. 1.5c, turned the branches upside down, left off the candles, and changed the base. The effect is rather startling. 2.37" **c.** This is a design that ART used again and again. It was offered in red, white, or green enamel and was also made as a pendant. You can see how this design reappears as a candle in Fig 4.3d and as a bell in Fig 5.12c. 2.25" $20-90 each.

Atwood & Sawyer (A&S). An English firm making high quality jewelry, gold or rhodium plated, and guaranteed against defects. They use Swarovski crystals.

Fig 1.8 Two trees by an English firm, Atwood & Sawyer, are signed on the back *A&S*. They are plated in 22 kt gold and carry a nonspecific guarantee "in the unlikely event of a manufacturing fault." These trees were purchased new at Harrod's in London. **a.** The Atwood tree for 1996. 1.87" **b.** 1997 edition. 1.62" $125-150 each.

Austria. This mark is no guarantee of the age of a piece. However, much of the jewelry signed Austria or Made in Austria is very good quality.

Fig 1.9 Both of these stunning trees are signed *Austria* in a small raised plaque, and all stones prong-set. **a.** Metal is gold-finished. Purchased new prior to 1962. 2.37" $45-110 **b.** Metal has been japanned, enhancing the tree's dramatic look. 1.5" $30-60

Fig 1.10 The stones of this breath-taking pin are set in a copper-colored metal, and many of the settings are open-backed. The multi-colored, decorative ornaments are pointed on the top and the candles are milky white. Signed *Austria* in a tiny plaque. 2.0" $45-110

Fig 1.11 From the front, these two trees appear nearly identical except for the two additional candles on the second. The candles on each are layered above the green rhinestone background, giving the pins extra depth. Each is signed *Made in Austria* on the pin bar and measures 2.37". **a.** Japanned metal. **b.** Pewter-colored metal. $115-165 each.

Fig 1.12 a. This tree is japanned, and nearly identical to the six-candle Weiss in Fig 1.161a. I know from collectors who bought Christmas jewelry in the 1950s and 1960s that this tree could be found signed either "Weiss" or "Made in Austria." The back of this example is japanned. (The Weiss can be found with either the standard gold back or with the japanned back.) 2.5" $125-200 **b.** A poorly crafted tree. Even the *Made in Austria* plaque on the back appears to be of lower quality. The surfaces are uneven and there are spaces between the stones, but the quality of the stones is excellent. 2.37" $65-110

Fig 1.13 A very unusual tree. Notice the four hanging crystal beads and the graduated rhinestone trunk. Some of the individual branches are bent slightly forward, giving the tree more depth. Signed *Austria* in a tiny plaque on the pin back. 2.5" $115-165

Fig 1.14 With enameled green front and back, this tree of deeply embossed evergreen foliage may have been made somewhat later than the others shown here. I believe the angel is original because it is attached with wiring that has been enameled the same green. I have never seen another Austria tree quite like this one. *Austria* embossed directly into the pin back. 3.87" $115-175

Avon.
Fig 1.15 First and second trees are signed *Avon* in an oval stamped directly into the tree. On the third, the signature appears in a raised oval. **a.** A lovely tree when worn on just about any color, the dark aurora borealis stones set off the gold bows nicely. This is the earliest of these three trees. **b.** Simple, woven design with a tiny rhinestone top. It measures just 1.25". **c.** This was new for Avon in 1983 and sold for $9.95. 2.12" $10-35 each.

Bauer. Dorothy Bauer has designed and manufactured rhinestone jewelry in Berkeley, California, since the middle of the 1980s. Many of her designs are available from one year to the next and are carried by dealers who specialize in Christmas jewelry. Bauer jewelry is also carried in a few upscale department stores.

Fig 1.16 These four pins are signed *Bauer* on an applied oval. All of these very glitzy trees were in production at the time of this writing. All can be found with a bale so they can be worn securely on a chain as a pendant. **a.** Stones are set deeply in a rich gold. Like much Bauer jewelry, this tree can be purchased in other colors. First offered in 1996. 2.25"
b. The Bauer candle tree. I also have this tree as a button cover: The back opens and slides over a button, so no pinback is needed. 2.0" **c.** Sometimes called "The Deco Tree," the stones are set in gold but Dorothy Bauer has also set it in silver. 1.75" **d.** The "Garland Tree" or "3-D Tree" is sometimes done in silver, more often in gold. It is occasionally found with other stone colors, but it is beautiful in any. 2.75" $25-80 each.

Fig 1.17 Five pins by Dorothy Bauer that are all current and sold with bales. **a.** Smaller flat design with a zigzag red garland layered above the tree. 1.75" **b.** A similar triangle with a few scattered ornaments, but with no the garland. Very glitzy, though simple. 1.37" **c.** Smallest size garland tree made, it is also made as a ring adjustable to fit any size finger. (There is a medium size- 2.12"- that is a standard tree.) This example is decorated in less commonly found colors. 1.62" **d.** A very simple triangle set in silver-colored metal. 1.5" **e.** This very effective, flat triangle with a huge top and extremely glittery stones also works well as a pendant. 2.5" $25-80 each.

Beatrix (BJ). This Providence, Rhode Island, company was formed in 1946 and took its name from the owner's sister, Beatrice. It got its start making Christmas tree pins and other holiday jewelry, then turned to animal jewelry. The company closed about 1983.

Fig 1.18 Four signed *Beatrix*. **a.** This is a triangle open to the back consisting of five tiers of four-petal flowers with a stone in each flower. 2.5" **b.** Cast in silver-colored metal, it consists of two layers. The back layer is green-foiled and the front layer is wires with settings strung between them, giving the tree an added dimension and reflection off the back. 2.5" **c.** This tree has only two settings, one in the trunk and one buried by the leaves. The remaining decoration is enamel poured in a framework; it looks a bit like stained glass. 2.75" **d.** Cheery green tree with three raised candy canes; cut open between green enameled sections. 2.5" $20-60 each.

Fig 1.19 A mixture of BJ and Beatrix. **a.** Silver metal with pale blue stones, signed *BJ*. The tree is composed of double rope-like loops. Notice that the pot has embossed leaves very much like Fig. 1.18a. This is a decoration used on some other BJ and Beatrix trees. 2.62" **b.** Cast in a pale gold color, delicate and old-fashioned-looking with four single, colored, rhine-stone garlands. 2.25" **c.** Signed *Beatrix*, but made by the same com-pany. Constructed of rope-like loops of wire, it appears to be nearly the same type figure as the first tree, but with each loop inverted. It is also cut open to the back. 2.37" **d.** A lovely, unusual, dark brass tree, signed *Beatrix*. Notice the stand for the base. The branches swoop down to star settings. 2.25" $20-55 each.

Fig 1.20 BJ (**b** and **c**) and Beatrix (**a** and **d**). **a.** This novel design has a ceramic front with a metal backing of the exact same shape glued to it. Its only stone is in the top—the two decorations visible at the middle of the tree are raised knobs. 1.87" **b.** Small, modern, open frame with three decorative rhinestones. 1.5" **c.** Clear rhinestones nearly cover this slightly curved surface, filling the space between five horizontal braids. 2.12" **d.** Enameled green with diagonal scalloped garlands and circular settings. 2.12" $15-50 each.

Benedict.

Fig 1.21 This nugget-like tree by Benedict is deeply textured and has three vertical grooves. Six unfaceted glass beads hang from loops and sixteen tiny red and green rhinestones are glued into the tree. 1.62" $45-90

Boucher. The mark was first used by jewelry designer Marcel Boucher, who immigrated to the United States from France in 1925. Later, jewelry was designed by Marcel and his wife, Sandra. The company continued in business until 1970.

Connie Bennett.

Fig 1.22 This tree is unsigned but was found on its original card that said it was "from the Connie Bennett collection." It is made of pieces of stained glass wrapped in copper and dipped in permanent gold plating. The top of the tree is a tiny gold angel. Pastel glass beads slide along the wiring, and there is even colored glass in the base. Each design is signed and copyrighted to protect the artist. The card stated that it is easy to care for—just wash in warm, soapy ammonia water. This is something you should never do with rhinestone jewelry! 3.62" $40-65

Fig 1.23 Two trees signed *Boucher*. Both are made in two layers and the back of each looks very much like Fig 2.46b. The stones on these trees are particularly tiny and include opaque, turquoise-colored stones, uncommon on Christmas trees. **a.** The tree sits planted on a turf-like base and is slightly open to the back and very delicate. 2.25" **b.** Four vertical drapes with stones down the center of each drape and the center of the tree. It sits on a tiny round base. 1.75" $40-70 each.

Brooks.

Fig 1.24 Three trees by Brooks. The first two are by far the more common and have harp-like strings **a**. A wide zigzag outline grooved to catch the harp-like wires. Four candles. 2.62" **b.** This is a smaller version without candles. 1.12" **c.** Much less common, a two-layer tree. The top layer is polished, the bottom is brushed. The trunk is a very long baguette candle with a clear tear-shaped flame. 2.5" $15-50 each.

Fig 1.25 This tree by Butler & Wilson is set in a silver metal background, which the prong-set stones and faux pearls completely cover. Purchased new in England in 1997. 3.12" $115-130

Butler & Wilson. An English firm that started its business in the late 1960s, and continues to manufacture jewelry today.

Cadoro. Manufacturer of high quality costume jewelry from 1955 until the early 1980s.

Carnegie, Hattie. Hattie Carnegie was a clothing designer and fashion doyen in the early part of the 20th Century. She expanded into the jewelry business rather late in her career, and her company continued to produce jewelry until the 1970s.

Fig 1.26 Two trees by Hattie Carnegie of very similar shape but made to look quite different. Each is a four-tier tree, the bottoms of which zig-zag. Each has a tracing of glitter that follows the cut at the tier bottom. Each measures 2.5." **a.** The stones appear to hang from the points of each tier, and more are embedded in the surface itself. Here the tree has a trunk and a simple, four-point star. **b.** This tree has been enameled a soft green. It grows from a rhinestone-rimmed pot and has a five-point, glittered star top and lovely navettes embedded in each tier. $75-140 each

Fig 1.27 a. The base of this Hattie Carnegie tree is a battery container. The top is a section of a cone with the stones set almost at surface level. If you buy a battery tree and think that you can use the battery, you may want to get some guarantee first, for it is seldom that you can find the right battery and the tree in working condition. Sometimes the tree's contacts are corroded. Usually you must look for a battery by trial and error. Consequently, I have never seen this tree working, but, working or not, it is lovely. 2.5" $40-75 **b.** A very unusual Hattie Carnegie tree that looks quite old. The garlands are covered with small rhinestones and there are a number of other stones decorating the tree. The effect is very lacey and fragile. 2.62" $95-150

Fig 1.28 Two with hanging beads signed *Hattie Carnegie*. Notice the similarity in the bead colors on these trees: each has a soft blue bead and an unusual milky colored bead, a ruby red, and a few others. **a.** If you wear this tree, you need never fear mashers. The branches are pointed and extend over half an inch from the trunk. It is enameled dark green and the trunk has a pointed, shiny stem. 2.0" **b.** A curved, solid, almost cone-sectioned tree with a deeply textured surface and the same hanging balls. 2.25" $135-185 each

Fig 1.29 Three trees by Carolee. The first and third are identical except for the coloring. **a.** Three-tiered tree with multicolored stones at the ends of the branches and a green enameled pot. 1.62" **b.** Now difficult to find, this was issued new in 1994 for $60. 2.25" **c.** With its red enameled pot, it was issued new for $75 in 1989. 1.62" $75-135 each

Carolee. Issued its first Christmas pins in 1987. There have been two limited editions—a snowman and tree, both in 1994. Carolee has continued to produce trees and other Christmas jewelry.

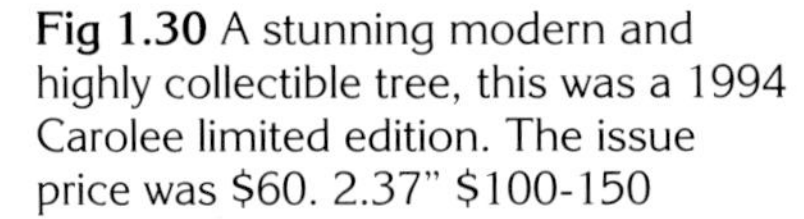

Fig 1.30 A stunning modern and highly collectible tree, this was a 1994 Carolee limited edition. The issue price was $60. 2.37" $100-150

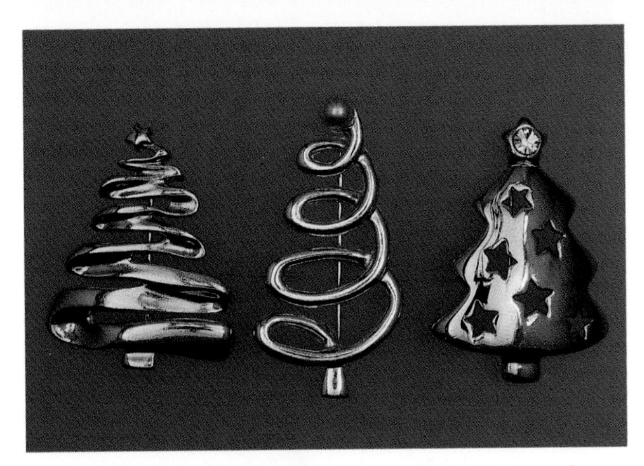

Fig 1.31 A set of three fairly recent Carolee trees of very modern designs. **a.** With no stones, this ribbon tree is simple and handsome. 1.62" **b.** This abstract tree is a continuous silver serpentine wire with a pearl top. 2.0" **c.** Flat, slightly rounded polished gold surface with stars cut through to the back. 2.0" $20-45 each

Castlecliff. Founded in the 1940s by Clifford Furst and sold only in the best stores. They continued jewelry production until the 1960s.

Fig 1.32 Three tiers of green-washed gold, three branches per tier; one lovely bead hangs from each branch. It is simple and elegant, by Castlecliff. 2.12" $40-80

Caviness, Alice. Jewelry from the 1940s to early 1960s. Like Hattie Carnegie, she began by manufacturing garments. Her work is highly regarded.

Corel. A division of Coro.

Fig 1.33 Three Corel trees. **a.** Five tiers of scallops, open between each tier. A raised gold braid trims the bottom of each scallop. 2.87" **b.** A tree of vertical ribbons with forms that look almost like flying birds. Some are set with tiny, clear rhinestones. 1.87" **c.** A five-tiered tree with the bottom edge of each tier cut in a zigzag through to the back. 2.75" $30-65 each

Fig 1.34 This Corel tree is an elegant floral design. It is as broad as it is tall, but cut-out areas give it a light and airy appearance. 2.0" $40-70

Fig 1.35 Two Corel trees, each enameled the same shade of green. **a.** Seven ribbon-like tiers of textured metal. Notice the rhinestones in the pot. The rest all hang from the tree bottom. 2.37" **b.** Six tiers of what look like inverted fans of pine needles interspersed with clear rhinestones and cut open slightly to the back. 2.12" $30-65 each

Coro. At one time, this was the largest manufacturer of costume jewelry in the country. This Providence, Rhode Island, company was in operation from 1919 to the1970s. Some of the output of this company was sold cheaply in variety stores. The two sisters who ran MYLU later joined Coro, where MYLU became a separate division in charge of Christmas and other holiday jewelry. The Coro group was also responsible for other labels, such as Corocraft, Corel, and Vendome.

Corocraft. Division of Coro.

Fig 1.36 Two elegant trees by Corocraft. **a.** Composed of diamond-shaped settings with the stones arranged by color to form diagonal patterns. Even the twisted trunk adds an interesting element. 2.5" **b.** Seven tiers of pearls graduated in size like a choker, all fitted on a curved triangular frame. 2.25" $40-90 each

Fig 1.37 Two light up by Corocraft. Each is shaped like the section of a cone; the battery fits into the back of the tree. Each 2.0" **a.** Slight hint of branches and deeper texture on this tree, into which multicolored navettes are embedded. Notice the twisted trunk. **b.** Has a pot for a base. This tree works with a 303 battery; if you have the tree, try one. $60-120 each

DeNicola. Founded in 1956, this name was not used after the early 1970s when the company was acquired by Capri.

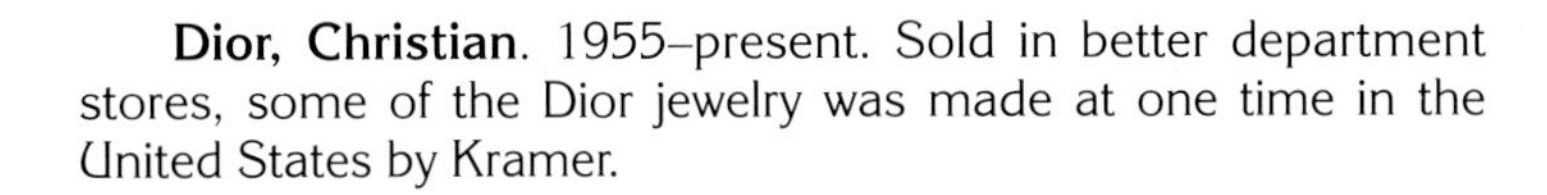

Dior, Christian. 1955–present. Sold in better department stores, some of the Dior jewelry was made at one time in the United States by Kramer.

Fig 1.39 Signed *Christian Dior*, this elegant tree is both modern and tailored. The surface is deeply textured to reflect the light. 2.0" $45-70

Fig 1.38 Three lovely trees by DeNicola. **a.** Metal is brushed gold; notice the baguette trim to the pot. I have also seen it with clear baguettes. Four solid tiers. 2.0" $40-75 **b.** An abstract, broad-leafed design with a very elaborate stand and treetop; cabochon stones. 2.62" $50-110 **c.** Seven vertical wires are attached at the bottom to a semi-circular frame, giving this tree considerable depth. Notice that the rhinestones are on and between the verticals. 1.87" $40-75

Dodds. The signature reads "DODDZ," but the company was begun by William Dodds in 1952. Collectors contributing to this book can remember making Dodds jewelry from kits purchased in the mid-1950s to the early 1980s from Jewel Creations.

Dominique. These trees are being made in the 1990s.

Eisenberg. Has made Christmas jewelry since sometime in the 1950s, not all of it signed. Current marked pieces will say either *Eisenberg* or *Eisenberg Ice*. The Christmas pins are carried by Marshall Field and other stores.

Fig 1.40 These trees by Dominique all are flat, composed of row after row of rhinestones. The interest is in their glitter and, in some cases, in the shape and color of the stones. **a.** A near triangle, with several stones attached almost randomly in a layer above the first. 2.87" **b.** Again, a nearly perfect triangle with a field of clear rhinestones bordered by colored rhinestones. The color of the border is reflected in the center stones, enhancing their effect. 2.0" **c.** In this case, spaces are left in the green background of the tree for the odd-shaped stones. Interesting flower-like star at the top. 3.5" $35-80 each

Fig 1.41 This tree was first issued by Eisenberg in the mid-'70s. It consists of a silver metal frame that holds a foil-backed, conic section of glass. Molded into the surface of the glass are vertical grooves and settings for the stones. It is rare to find this tree with the foil perfectly intact. 2.25" $250-375

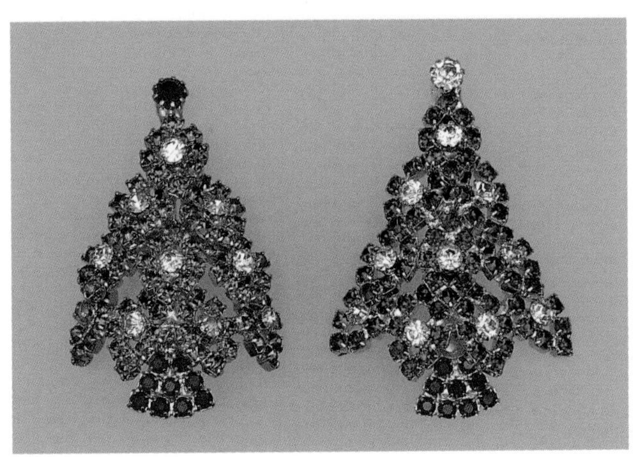

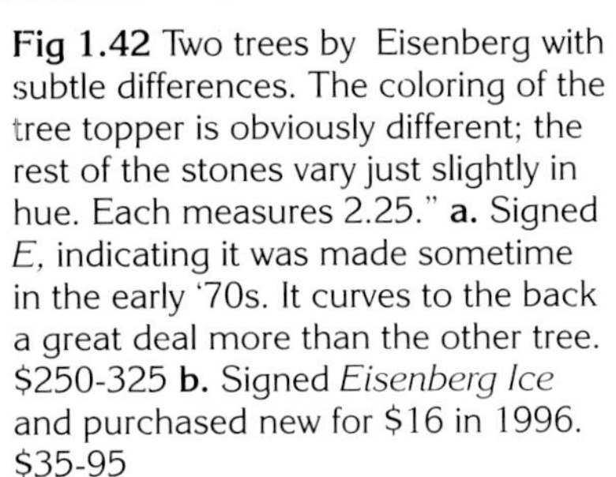

Fig 1.42 Two trees by Eisenberg with subtle differences. The coloring of the tree topper is obviously different; the rest of the stones vary just slightly in hue. Each measures 2.25." **a.** Signed *E,* indicating it was made sometime in the early '70s. It curves to the back a great deal more than the other tree. $250-325 **b.** Signed *Eisenberg Ice* and purchased new for $16 in 1996. $35-95

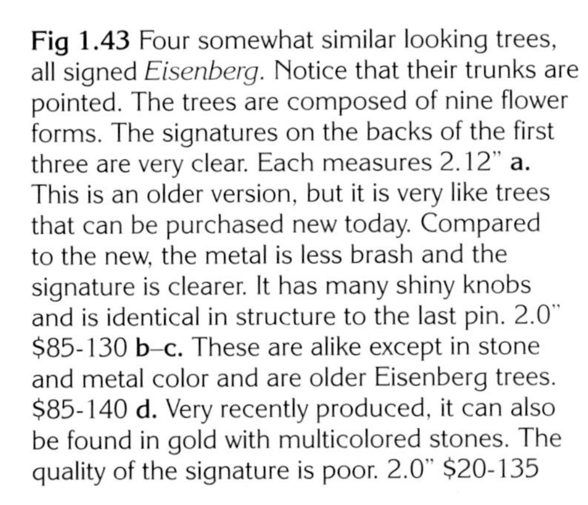

Fig 1.43 Four somewhat similar looking trees, all signed *Eisenberg*. Notice that their trunks are pointed. The trees are composed of nine flower forms. The signatures on the backs of the first three are very clear. Each measures 2.12" **a.** This is an older version, but it is very like trees that can be purchased new today. Compared to the new, the metal is less brash and the signature is clearer. It has many shiny knobs and is identical in structure to the last pin. 2.0" $85-130 **b–c.** These are alike except in stone and metal color and are older Eisenberg trees. $85-140 **d.** Very recently produced, it can also be found in gold with multicolored stones. The quality of the signature is poor. 2.0" $20-135

Fig 1.44 More versions of the Eisenberg tree with knobs. **a.** In silver, with all-blue stones, it tarnishes. Nonetheless, it is a new tree. 2.0" **b.** Although only a little shorter, it appears considerably smaller than the first tree. It is much less common, with fewer stones. It is also in silver that tarnishes. 1.87" $15-45 each

Fig 1.45 This tree was made in 1994 as a part of the Eisenberg classic series. It was a limited edition: only eighty were made in this color combination—rose-lavender rhinestone navettes and green round stones. Eighty more were made in the reverse combination (green navettes and rose-lavender round stones). The aurora borealis effect makes it difficult to see the actual stone color. This large and magnificent tree is very difficult to find. The pin is signed *Eisenberg Ice – 1994*. It was issued in 1994 for $125. 3.0" $350-650

Fig 1.46 Prong-set stones almost completely cover both of these Eisenberg Ice trees. **a.** Six baguette candles. First issued in 1992. The large colored ornaments on this slightly domed tree make it particularly handsome. 2.37" $35-95 **b.** Somewhat smaller, similar tree with four baguette candles and three large ornaments, a recent release. 1.75" $15-40

Fig 1.47 Five trees, each signed *Eisenberg Ice*. **a.** A tree made of five tiers of scallops. One stone decorates each scallop. This tree is a fairly recent issue. 2.0" **b.** A tree of three tiers with zigzag bottom with stones embedded in it. Issued in 1988 but recently still available in some department stores. 2.0" **c.** Notice the similarity to the ART garland trees Fig 1.4c, even to the zigzag on the pot and the placement of ornaments on the garlands. 2.12" **d.** Green enameled tree in brown enameled pot. I am unsure of the issue date. It is divided into small scalloped sections by gold rope garlands. One clear rhinestone decorates each scallop. 2.12" **e.** Another very common design found with the signatures like "H (in a heart)" and Kramer. Three tiers, lacey interior and a varying number of stones—this one has nine. 1.87" $15-30 each

Fig 1.48 Each of these is signed *Eisenberg Ice*. **a.** This was issued new at $45 for Christmas of 1997. The large stones are aurora borealis and their color is picked up in the clear stones as well. 2.12" $45 **b.** Tiny, antique brass tree with stones separated by clusters of brass knobs. New in 1997, it is a very effective treatment in a brass pot. 1.75" $20-40 **c.** Composed entirely of long, green, brilliant navettes. It was issued new for Christmas of 1996 for $80. 3.0" $80

Ferrá, Marie. I could learn nothing about this manufacturer.

Fig 1.49 Stones completely cover this very large and magnificent four- or five-layer tree by Marie Ferrá. The effect of the clear rhinestones surrounding the green navettes and the many ornaments on such a large tree is simply dazzling. It was new for Christmas of 1993 and sold at stores like Niemann-Marcus and Saks Fifth Avenue for $375. 3.75" $400+

Florenza. This design firm was in operation for just a few years in the later 1950s and early 1960s. They did not manufacture jewelry but sold their designs to jobbers.

Fig 1.50 With four tiers of short, fat, individual wires of a deep brass color, this tree by Florenza is more substantial than delicate. 2.37" $60-120

Fig 1.51 This tree by Florenza is as delicate as the last was substantial—three tiers of filigreed loops, each enclosing a dangling pearl. 2.62" $35-75

Gerry's. Has been making Christmas jewelry from the 1950s to present. Current designs, modestly priced, are featured during the holidays in stores such as Target and Caldor.

Fig 1.52 Five trees by Gerry's. Each has only one stone, and that in the top star. **a.** Seven to eight tiers of small, inverted fans with one colored knob on each fan cut to the back between. 2.37" **b.** Four tiers of medium-size, inverted fans, each decorated with a row of knobs at the bottom. Open to the back. 2.37" **c.** On this, the most recently issued and widely available of these trees, fan-like shapes form a solid tree, with one knob to each fan. 2.0" **d.** Open, diagonally feathery, light green branches with colored knobs swoop upward from left to right. 2.12" **e.** Four to five tiers of garlands, open between. The colored knobs bridge the garlands. 2.0" $3-30 each

Giovanni.
Fig 1.53 These trees were photographed together because of their obvious similarities. The left side of each is concave, the right side convex. Each has a slender trunk ending in a clean cut visible to the front. **a.** Although this tree is signed, the signature is unreadable. 2.5" **b.** Sleek, tailored and unadorned by stones, this tree relies on its form for its beauty. Signed *Giovanni*. 2.75" $40-85 each

Gold Crown Inc.
Fig 1.54 Here is a particularly bold design with unusual glass settings. The three large settings are glass disks with intaglio silver stars. The frame is very tall and thin. Gold Crown Inc. See a variation in Fig 1.187d. 2.75" $20-45

H (in a heart). This mark (a flowing heart inscribed with a capital *H*) appears on a number of Christmas trees. The mark has been found with the letters *edy* outside the heart. It has been determined that this is a variation of the Hedy mark. The manufacturer was Hedison. (See also page 34 for Hedy.)

Fig 1.55 All three pieces are signed with an *H* within a *heart*. This may be a signature of Hedy (see notes above). **a.** This same design has been done with many different signatures. Sometimes the number of tiers or the number of stones varies from as few as sixteen to as many as forty stones on other versions of this tree. 2.25" **b.** Notice the dramatic effect that a black frame can add to a tree. The design is simple enough, a variation on the first tree, but the effect is achieved by the color of the stones against the black background. 2.12" **c.** A tree of diamond shapes, some textured with a green wash and some open with amber stones. This tree is 2.5" $15-55 each

Hagler. Stanley Hagler, who designed and made beaded jewelry, died in 1996. His designs and mark have recently been used by a former employee. There is great demand for his Christmas trees.

Fig 1.56 Signed *Stanley Hagler N.Y.C.* Each of these trees consists of more than one layer of metal. They are beautiful when viewed from the back as well as from the front. Both consist of beads strung to the tree and prong-set rhinestones. **a.** A framework like an open, broad-leaf branch with flowers and stones on each leaf. If you turn the pin sidewise, you can see the wiring that strings the beads to the front layer. The front frame is then wired to the identical back layer. The small, petal-like stones are all prong-set rhinestones. 3.12" **b.** Made in several layers, the largest jade green stones are glued, the smaller red stones are prong-set. What appear to be tiny stones are actually glass beads. 2.75" $95-350 each

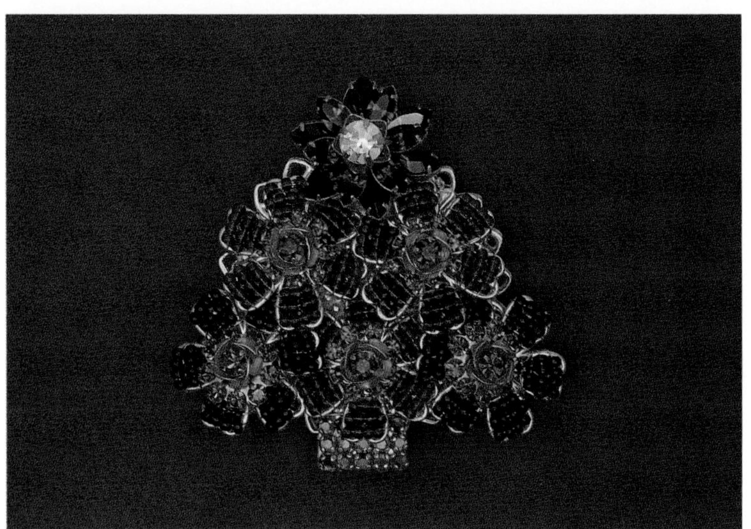

Fig 1.57 This tree by Stanley Hagler is constructed similarly to Fig 1.56b, but some of the details are different. In addition to the different coloration, the base is not beaded but consists of rows of prong-set stones. The center stone in each flower is prong-set and is surrounded by a row of prong-set stones. The most striking difference, however, is the multi-level star at the top, consisting of two layers of prong-set navettes topped by an unusual five-pointed star cup holding a clear aurora borealis stone. 2.25" $95-350

Hedy. These designs were created by Hedison, a Providence, Rhode Island, area manufacturer in the 1960s and 1970s. It is now closed. (See also page 33 for H (in a heart).)

Fig 1.58 Four trees by Hedy. **a.** Eleven star-bursts open to the back between them are set in a pot. 2.5" **b.** Four tiers of vertical green ribbons with gold scalloped borders at each tier. The ornaments appear to hang from the garlands. 2.12" **c.** A tree of open diamonds connected by knobs. The stones are centered in each diamond and are of unusual colors. 2.12" **d.** Feathery branches over a trunk with four roots. The stones are glued into little five-pointed star settings. 2.25" $20-50 each

Hobé. 1887–present. Originating in Paris but now located in Mount Vernon, New York, Hobé has made Christmas jewelry since about the 1950s.

Fig 1.59 Two trees by Hobé. **a.** Prong-set rhinestones cover the frame of this multi-layered tree, which is open to the back. The pearls hang free, just touching the bottoms of the layers, giving the tree a shimmering effect. 2.75" **b.** A rather free-form, deeply textured tree with many projections. Seven translucent, red beads hang from some of the projections. 1.75" $85-145 each

Fig 1.60 Five trees signed *Hobé*. **a.** Stones cover the five tiers of branches; each branch is cut to the trunk. The tree is nearly flat and is green, except for the few scattered ornaments. 2.0" $65-135 **b.** This tree is large and deep. It is outlined in green navettes. In the center are mounded iridescent beads with tiny beads at their centers. 3.0" $125-$185 **c.** An unusual, lacey border surrounds this tree's navette center. The stones are all prong-set, including the ornaments around the outside of the scrollwork. 1.87" $50-110 **d.** Small, stone-covered tree of diagonal branches alternating in color. 1.62" $20-50

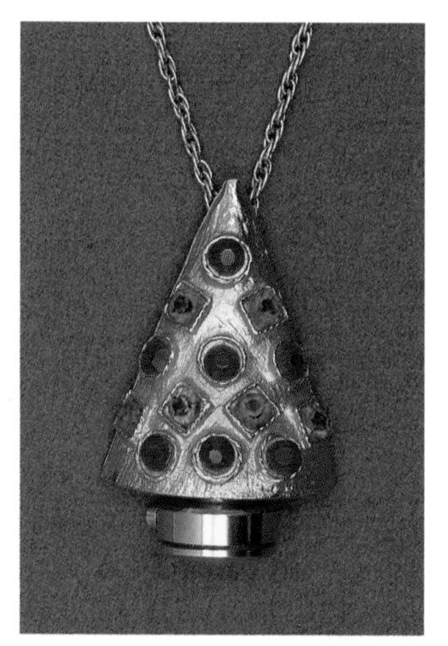

Fig 1.61 This is not a pin but a pendant. It is a battery tree shaped like a section of a cone. The battery fits into the base. Signed *Hobé*. 1.87" $85-150

Hollycraft. This producer began life as Hollywood Jewelry in 1948 and flourished until 1978. It was one of those that designed jewelry that it contracted with jobbers to manufacture. Often identifiable by the use of pastel or non-primary colored stones. Hollycraft also made jewelry for Pakula, Kramer, and Weiss.

Fig 1.62 Dazzling siam red aurora borealis stones float above textured garland loops on this potted tree by Hollecraft. Look for this beautifully designed flowerpot on other Hollycraft trees. The top star is a flat-topped red rhinestone. 2.5" $70-150

Fig 1.63 Three candle trees by Hollycraft. The first two are quite similar, each having the same number of candles, which are stones pointed only at the upper end. The pots and the draping are identical. **a.** This has nearly jet-black candles, red, green and amber ornaments in garland-like rows. 2.37" **b.** Deep rose candles and red and green ornaments. This tree has fewer ornaments because every other setting is a cluster of tiny brass knobs. 2.37" **c.** Here the candles are all vertical navettes that sit above ropey loops in a square-slatted pot. 2.25" $75-175 each

Fig 1.64 Three by Hollycraft. The tree pins are identical except for color. Both are outline trees comprising two layers of slightly drooping branches, barely bent forward. They are decorated with lovely, flat-backed rhinestones. Notice that the pot is the same as in Fig 1.62. Each is 2.37" **a.** These clip-on earrings match the first tree pin. The tree hangs from a small brass medallion. 1.25" $20-40 **b.** Bright brass finish and pastel rhinestones. $45-110 **c.** Enameled white metal with milky aurora borealis stones. $85-160

Fig 1.65 Two trees and a pair of earrings by Hollycraft. These are the only Hollycraft trees I know of that have dangling beads. The branches are quite sharp and pointed, like a bare evergreen, and could certainly inflict injury in a fond embrace. This tree is very open. Both trees are 2.5" **a.** There are faceted red and green aurora borealis stones with a clear rhinestone in the star top. $135-225 **b.** Tiny earrings with four faceted dangles that match the second tree. These earrings are unsigned, but there is no place for a signature on the back. 1.25" $60-110 **c.** Identical to the first tree, but with variously colored aurora borealis faceted beads. $135-225

Fig 1.66 Here are three Hollycraft trees that are more commonly found. **a.** Five vertical strips of deeply scored metal, three forward and two back, are decorated with fourteen flat-back rhinestones in two sizes. There is one more in the star top. It is sometimes found in red, green, and clear stones, something that is not uncommon for Hollycraft trees. It has an inverted bowl stand. 2.25" **b.** This tree is brass, but it is sometimes found in a very light gold finished metal. I've seen it with green baguettes in the trunk. It is a two-layer tree with the branches cut nearly to the trunk. The branches are not bent forward. It has four small baguette candles, a two-baguette trunk, and twenty-four round rhinestones, including the one in the star top. 2.25" **c.** A tree that has been copied over and over again, but the copies are never as lovely as the original. It is a very broad triangle of frosty brass with open vertical slits, crisscrossed by four garlands of clear rhinestones alternating with brass knobs. 2.37" For copies see Fig 2.48. $45-140 each

Fig 1.67 Two Hollycraft trees very much alike except in color. Each tree has six candles, eight round ornaments, and drooping, feathery branches that are slightly open to the back. Each has a many-pointed metal star at the top and is 2.37" tall. **a.** Finished in a bright brass, the candles on this tree are clear baguettes and the flames are red rhinestones. The six largest ornament stones are pointed on top; the lowest two of these are watermelon tourmaline. **b.** The candles are painted metal and the flames are milky aurora borealis. The ornament stones are a combination of milky and clear aurora borealis stones without pointed tops. $85-190 each

Fig 1.68 Two Hollycraft trees identical except for the coloration. Both are brass. Between the garlands the ornaments appear to hang in filigree settings. Each is 2.25." **a.** White enameled garlands. **b.** Garlands of red enameling. $135-200 each

Fig 1.69 Two trees identical except for their color. Each has seventeen stones and is 2.25." The drapes beneath the stones are a lovely filigree pattern. **a.** A pewter-colored metal unusual for Hollycraft. All rhinestones are a pale blue. **b.** Brass metal. Stones are blue with a pink stripe down the center, something I have seen only in Hollycraft Christmas jewelry. $85-140 each

Fig 1.70 A lovely Hollycraft tree with faux opals decorating abstract wire-thread boughs. There are also six tiny pearls ornaments. 2.25" $125-190

Fig 1.71 Two trees by Hollycraft. **a.** Six tiers of seven petal flowers, each with a rhinestone center. A few additional stones are scattered between the flowers and the lower half of the tree. The brass petals are decorated with tiny knobs. The tree is slightly open to the back. Here, with variously colored stones. 2.37" $85-160 **b.** I think of this as the "teepee tree," with a theme of inverted cut-through *V*s repeated down the tree. It is made in three separate tiers, each with a row of small stones above a row of larger stones. The rhinestone colors, as on many Hollycraft trees, are a mix of primary and unusual secondary and tertiary colors. 2.37" $85-130

Fig 1.74 A set by Hollycraft. **a.** These clip-back earrings match the tree, though the match would be better with stones of other colors. The tiny trees dangle from a filigreed knob with a green rhinestone center. 1.25" $20-45 **b.** The tree is of dark-toned brass with droopy, rope-like branches separated by rhinestones in various sizes and colors. It curves slightly to the back. 2.25" $65-110

Fig 1.72 These two Hollycraft trees are identical in every way to those in Fig 1.71 except for stone color. Here, the stones are entirely dark red and deep green, enhancing the dramatic effect. I wonder whether these trees were marketed in both color combinations during the same year. Clear aurora borealis stones at the top are very common in Hollycraft trees. Each measures 2.37" **a.** $85-160 **b.** $60-130

Fig 1.73 Three more Hollycraft trees done in the red and green theme. **a.** For obvious reasons, this tree is often called the "bow-tie tree." I have only seen it done in red and green, though sometimes it comes without enamel. Notice the beautiful detail-work on the pot of this tree. 2.25" **b.** This tiny tree is a solid-backed and slightly curved; it alternates rows of red and green stones in bezel-like settings. The trunk is a tiny baguette. 1.25" **c.** More common tree by Hollycraft, sometimes found with multicolored stones. This tree is solid with raised beaded garlands and five raised baguette candles with rhinestone flames. There are additional ornaments along the bottom and scattered on the tree. 2.25" For an unsigned copy, see Fig 2.4b. $45-110 each

Fig 1.77 An unusual, almost primitive metalwork design by Hollycraft. The frame looks hand-hammered. The tree has seven long, clear, baguette candles with enameled flames and seventeen additional ornaments. 2.37"
See two more examples of this tree, one by Pakula Fig 1.127 and one unsigned Fig 2.40a.
$85-150

Fig 1.75 A Hollycraft set. The tree has very spikey branches that point upward, reminiscent of Charlie Brown's scraggly Christmas tree. With its ornaments, however, it is anything but an ugly duckling. **a.** Clip-back earrings (they do not dangle). 1.12" $35-60 **b.** Tall, nearly flat tree in a square planter box with vertical slats. 2.37" $70-135

Fig 1.76 These two Hollycraft trees are nearly alike—the color of their metal is the most obvious difference. Both have opalescent stones in star tops. Their large ornament stones sit above double rope drapes. 2.5" each
a. Fifteen milky, aurora borealis stones plus one in the top. It has metal knobs between the large stones, where the brass tree has small ornaments. **b.** Brass with fifteen large multicolored rhinestones and eleven more tiny stones. $60-180 each

Fig 1.78 This triangular, shaggy, picture-frame border encloses settings for odd-shaped and colored stones of all sorts. The tear-shaped stone at the bottom has a textured surface. You can see through this Hollycraft tree very slightly. 2.25" $85-190

Fig 1.80 This lattice-work tree by Hollycraft is open to the back. The centers of the fifteen diamonds are square-shaped stones, flat on top, each mounted with a corner pointing toward the top of the tree. The tree topper is a clear rhinestone. 2.37" $60-130

Fig 1.81 This is a tiny look-alike version of the tree in Fig 1.66b. It has eight branches on each side and is made in two layers, with just two little baguette candles and a one-baguette trunk. 1.5" $45-110

Fig 1.79. **a.** The two-tiered, clip-on earrings in this Hollycraft set have seven flat-backed ornaments in two sizes. 1.2" $45-85 **b.** Four tiers of petal-like projections, each tier with a rope garland at the bottom and vertical slits. It sits in a lovely scalloped pot. There are fifteen flat-back rhinestones in all. 2.5" $45-130 **c.** Sometimes called the "ribbon tree" for its many layers of long, curved, ribbon-like branches, each adorned with alternating stones and knobs. This tree is also beautiful in red and green. 2.37" $55-140

Fig 1.82 Three Hollycraft trees. **a.** This is identical to Fig 1.80 except that the stones are round and flat-topped. 2.37" $60-130 **b.** The four tiers have textured gold borders and deep-set, flat-topped red and green rhinestones. Notice that the pot is the same as on the first tree. 2.37" $60-145 **c.** Six skirt-like tiers cut clear back to the trunk. The ornaments appear to hang from the bottom of each tier. There are twenty-six stones in all, including the clear aurora borealis at the top. 2.37" $75-185

Fig 1.83 This Hollycraft is similar to Fig 1.82b, except that clusters of tiny brass knobs replace the top row of stones. The stones are not flat-topped. Notice that the end stone in tier three is blue with a pink stripe. 2.25" $60-145

Fig 1.84 Collectors argue whether Hollycraft intended this as a tree, but they seek it avidly, nonetheless. It is the only prong-set Hollycraft "tree" and the only one dated on the back, *Hollycraft COPR. 1950*. Here is the sort of truly pastel colors so characteristic of this designer. The scroll metal work is lovely. Most of the foiled stones are open to the back. 1.75" $85-145

Fig 1.85 Buyer beware! This tree, purchased new at Christmas 1997 for $18 from J. B. White department store, represents what Christmas tree collectors have dreaded. Until now, we could be certain that a tree signed Hollycraft was old. This tree bears an official-looking signature and is brand new. It is a very pretty tree; the white metal front and back are covered with tiny, glued-on faux pearls, but you won't want to pay the price of an old Hollycraft. 1.75" $18

Jack, Judith. A current jewelry designer whose work is featured in fine jewelry stores and a few upscale department stores.

Fig 1.86 Both of these trees are sterling and are marked *Judith Jack*. They were purchased in 1996 from retail stores. I have learned that every year Judith Jack makes a new Christmas tree, which is carried by a few department stores and some fine jewelers. **a.** In a silver pot, a tree of five tiny silver tiers of branches; six red and green cabochon ornaments adorn the surface. 1.5" **b.** The ornaments on this more deeply textured tree are raised silver. It sits in a bright green, enameled pot with an enameled red bow at the top. 1.62" $55-75 each

JJ. This signature is used by Jonette Jewelry, which has been producing lovely Christmas pins since the late 1940s. Their newer pins can be found at stores like Sears and Casual Corner.

Fig 1.87 Three trees by JJ. Notice the jagged-cut trunk and red rhinestone treetops, common characteristics of JJ trees. **a.** This is an unusual and beautiful tree of undulating broadleaf branches, tiny clusters of brass knobs, large faux pearls, and tiny stones. It has nineteen pearls and twenty-one deep-set stones, plus its top stone. 2.5" $60-100 **b.** Small tree of open, dark brass scrolls of rope and just a few scattered ornaments, all of the same size. 1.87" $30-50 **c.** Notice how this lovely tailored tree resembles the Weiss tree, Fig 1.173. The placement and number of garlands is different, but the green wash is identical. All of the rhinestones are on the garlands. 2.5" $25-55

Fig 1.88 Three JJ trees. **a.** Broad curved triangle cut by four diagonal garlands of large, bright rhinestones and five diagonal rows of cut-through stars. All the stones are on the garlands. 2.25" **b.** A tree cut by seven short garlands of stones. The surprising thing is that this is the same basic tree as Fig 1.87c. Here with the brushed finish, the effect is startlingly different. 2.5" **c.** A smaller, three-tier tree, lattice cut. Rows of colored stones alternate with knobs, and they are separated by rows of tiny stars. 2.25" $30-55 each

Fig 1.89 Three by JJ. **a.** The two-tier earrings that go with the first tree. 1.25" $20-35 **b.** Seven tiers are cut open between drooping feather-like leaves. The tip of each leaf is split and holds a small, colored rhinestone. 2.37" $30-55 **c.** Notice the similarity of this tree to Weiss 1.176c—although the petals on the projections on this tree have tiny projections on them, they are cut between and swoop out, just like the Weiss petals. 2.37" $30-55

Fig 1.90 Three JJ trees. **a.** This is a common JJ tree shape, but the solid surface has shiny, embossed leaf patterns set with twenty tiny stone ornaments. 2.12" **b.** This very broad tree, cut to the back, is composed of wavy horizontal sections with tiny stones. Notice the use of purple stones here and in many of the JJ trees. 2.25" **c.** Here is a latticework of diamonds, each tier adding one more diamond—2twenty-nine all total. The stones are suspended in the center of each diamond. 2.12" $20-50 each

1.92 All by JJ. **a.** The three-tier, three-garland earrings that go with the first tree. 1.25" $20-40 **b.** Six separate tiers decorated with five loose, single-colored garlands of rhinestones. Notice that the pot for this tree and the next are identical and their tree structures are nearly identical. 2.25" $30-60 **c.** Six separate, deeply scored, green-washed tiers decorated with a few small rhinestone ornaments make this an effective tree. 2.37" $20-40

Fig 1.91 a. Garlands cut this typically broad JJ shape into eleven partial tiers. The clear rhinestone garlands give it a tailored look. 2.25" **b.** Eleven tiny baguette candles with enamel flames and small ornaments decorate the only JJ candle tree I know of. 2.12" **c.** An elegant JJ design employing branch outlines and thin branches of rhinestones open to the back. 2.37" $30-60 each

Fig 1.93 More by JJ. **a.** A three-tiered tree cut through by six circles, each filled with six small rhinestones. 2.25" **b.** Seven half-tiers with ropey bottoms cut this tree to the back. The tiers are decorated with round stones, navettes, and pear-shaped stones. 2.12" **c.** This curved, nearly solid tree is decorated with large navettes at the bottom tips of each of three tiers, which are slightly cut out and tilted from its surface. 2.37" $30-65 each

Fig 1.94 a. Three diagonal sections, each cut by long, vertical loops that contain the settings for this tree. Notice the shaggy, rooted trunk and the typical JJ shape to this tree. 2.25" **b.** This bears some resemblance to JJ Fig 1.88a, except that the diagonals go the opposite way and the sections between, instead of being solid, are cut with vertical bars. This is a very handsome tree in the dark, more antique shade of gold. 2.37" **c.** Here is a JJ triangle composed of short, lacey swags with clusters of stones in the openings between the swags. There are twenty-seven stones in all. 2.25" $30-50 each

Fig 1.95 Three smaller size green trees by JJ. **a.** Three tiers, open to the back between the tiers, with bottom rope garlands that loop up to form openings that hold the stones—one in each of six rope loops. 1.87" **b.** A tree of wavy, vertical strands with six openings for the stone settings. Including the top, there are seven stones on this 2.0" tree. **c.** Three solid green tiers (cut through between) with gold braid bottoms. There are ten tiny ornament stones. 1.75" $20-35 each

Fig 1.96 Three small trees by JJ. **a.** Three separate tiers, each cut with thin, vertical, oblong slits. The settings for the stones are between the slits. 1.75" **b.** Identical to Fig 1.95a, but of uncolored metal. 1.75" **c.** Three separate tiers have scalloped bottoms and oval openings. Seven stones, one at the top and one in each opening. 1.75" $20-35 each

Top center: **Fig 1.97** Five by JJ. **a.** A lovely antique brass triangle with six stones around its perimeter and a very large oval cabochon at its center. 2.0" **b.** Simple garland-cut triangle. Each section is adorned with one colored rhinestone in a star-shaped setting. 1.75" **c.** This tree is cut by three tiers with zigzag bottoms. The stones appear to hang from the bottom tips on each tier. 1.87" **d.** Feather-like branches, open to the back between, form this slightly curved triangular tree. Twenty-three colored rhinestones, including the one at the top, decorate it. 2.37" **e.** Each branch here is a single four-lobed leaf. Enameled orange-red knobs serve as ornaments; a single, red aurora borealis rhinestone adorns the star at the top. Unusual for JJ is the flower pot base. 2.0" $20-45 each

Top right: **Fig 1.98**. All by JJ. **a.** This tree is composed of five solid, separate, undulating tiers with very shaggy bottom edges plated in a light gold color. There are some raised knobs and nineteen stones, including the top. 2.37" **b.** A praying angel forms the top of this tree. The spiral branches on which the stones rest are her skirt. 2.0" **c.** Five separate layers with scalloped, beaded bottoms and serpentine cuts running through each layer. The twelve stones on this tree are separated by raised, gold knobs. 2.25" $20-40 each

Bottom right: **Fig 1.99** These two trees are very recent JJ productions. **a.** In this amusing pin for any cat fancier, two cats take delight in their own fantasy of the perfect Christmas tree. 3.25" **b.** An unusual and graceful abstract design combines two effective ideas in one tree. 2.5" $15-30 each

Kirk's Folly. Since 1979, a family-owned business with two separate lines of jewelry: available on Quality Value Channel, and the larger portion of its Christmas jewelry from individual retailers. They produce both open stock and limited edition pieces. The first Limited Edition Christmas tree was offered in 1992. They also have a newsletter and have started a collectors club offering special limited edition jewelry.

Fig 1.100 Twenty stars, half of them covered with tiny rhinestones, hang from this showy, very large, limited edition tree. The plaque on the back says *Kirk's Folly* and it gives the number—in this case 220 of a total edition of 300. The tree itself comprised seven tiers of open loops of green rhinestones, all prong-set, each containing a large, red, prong-set stone. The overall height is 5.25" $80-150

Fig 1.101 Chains of rhinestones dangle freely from this five-tiered Kirk's Folly tree of iridescent stones. The back indicates that it is one of a limited edition of 300 and it states the number of the particular tree. This tree was done in several other colors, including green and clear chains of rhinestones. This pin was available in 1997; the green one also comes in a smaller size. This one is 3.37" $70-175

Fig 1.102 Both of these large Kirk's Folly trees are from editions limited to 500, as marked on the back. Both have large, heart-shaped stones as the central part of their decorations. **a.** Double loops of green rhinestones enclose the large, red stones. The tree is planted in a pot. 3.87" $70-185 **b.** Here, the heart-shaped stones are contained in open heart-shaped rims of stones. The rhinestone at the top is heart-shaped and pointed in the center. 2.87" $65-185

Fig 1.103 Three modest pewter-colored trees, all currently available from Kirk's Folly dealers. **a.** The tiny stones look like shooting stars on this five-tiered tree. Four toys dangle from the bottom. 2.87" **b.** The basic structure of this tree is very much like the ART tree Fig 1.4a. However, it has more stones, 6 small fixed stars, and five three-dimensional hanging stars with pearls in their centers. The fixed stars are centered with stones, and all of the stones except the pearls are clear aurora borealis. 2.37" **c.** Another tree with hanging toys at the bottom. The tree is so heavily decorated with dangling, milky, faceted beads, six-pointed star snowflakes, and both clear and aurora borealis stones that you can hardly see the five separate tiers behind. 2.87" $10-30 each

Fig 1.104 Two pewter-colored trees by Kirk's Folly. **a.** The basic structure of this tree is identical to Fig 1.103b, but the stars are fixed and some of them are stone-covered. All stars are in a separate layer on top of the tree itself. 2.37" **b.** This pin consists of fifteen identical angels, each holding at least one, sometimes two stars with clear rhinestone centers. 2.25" $12-30 each

Fig 1.105 a. This was the first Limited Edition tree produced in 1992 by Kirk's Folly. None of the hanging stars have rhinestones and it is a limited edition of three hundred trees. 2.75" $140-200 **b.** Identical to Fig 1.103a except that there are only three toys hanging from the bottom. Because this tree was purchased second-hand, it is difficult to know whether one toy is missing or whether it was made that way. 2.75" $12-25

Fig 1.106 Two by Kramer. **a.** This tree can be found in a number of color combinations. Here it is in white metal with gold highlights. It consists of six skirt-like tiers, each extending back to the trunk and each decorated with alternating clear and aqua vertical baguettes. 2.37" $65-140 **b.** This tree in shiny gold is the same as Fig 1.55b, but without the black frame. Even the unusual chartreuse rhinestones are used again in this tree, making me feel that the same jobber produced it for both Kramer and "H in a Heart." The stones here, fifty-four in all, are a mix of clear iridescent and a few sparkly ornaments. 2.12" $45-85

Kramer. Founded in 1943 and not marketed since the late 1970s. This New York company also produced some jewelry for Christian Dior.

Fig 1.107 Two trees by Kramer. **a.** Like Fig 1.106b, except here it has a light, bright gold finish and traditional red and green stones. 2.37" $65-145 **b.** Also in Christmas colors, this tree is entirely made of rhinestones deeply embedded in a rich, gold-toned setting. 2.25" $45-100

Lane, Kenneth J. 1963–present. He has designed a few Christmas trees.

Fig 1.108 Two trees by Kenneth Lane. **a.** This appears to be an older tree, set in silver metal with stones covering its three tiers of swooping branches. 2.87" $40-100 **b.** This slightly open triangle comprises four tiers of flower-like objects. The center of each is a smooth, milky navette. 2.75" $40-85

Fig 1.110 Enameled green front and back, this tree by Lisner is made in two layers of thirteen circles of needles. Pastel, tear-shaped rhinestones set the tree off magnificently. 2.25" $50-95

Lisner. 1938–present. It is not certain when they made Christmas jewelry.

Fig 1.109 Two by Lisner. **a.** Two layers of deep-cut branches, five to a side, decorated with oversized ornaments. Notice the three pearls in the base of this tree. 2.12" **b.** The branches of this two-layer tree have tiny knobs that make it look as if it has been touched with frost. The ornaments appear to hang from the branches. It grows in a pretty, delicate pot. 2.0" $50-110 each

LJM. Nothing seems to be recorded about this company.

Lunch at the Ritz. This line of jewelry is not available in department stores. You will find pieces in gift or specialty stores and through some jewelry dealers who only sell at shows. The enamel is particularly durable because it is coated with epoxy resin.

Fig 1.111 Four trees by LJM. **a.** Four scalloped tiers of open, lacey filigree work are decorated with eight clear or red aurora borealis stones. 2.0" **b.** At first glance this resembles the smaller Brooks tree Fig 1.24b. On closer examination, with the two trees in hand, you can see that the Brooks is carefully strung to grooves in the outer edges, whereas the wires of the LJM are wrapped, often missing the grooves. Its stones are glued in, whereas in the Brooks they are prong-set. 2.25" **c.** This looks a bit like a JJ in shape and trunk. It is a triangle with six rope garlands and vertical slits. 2.37" **d.** Which came first, this or the very similar Pell Fig 1.132a? This tree, decorated with just thirteen red and green baguettes, measures 2.37" $20-40 each

Fig 1.112 If you want to get attention or start a conversation, this may be your solution. At 3.0" and many dangles, this is a beautifully done contemporary tree by Lunch at the Ritz. The enamel is resin-coated to give it durability. The rhinestone garlands that crisscross the tree may not be obvious in the photo. $200-230

Mamselle. From 1962–

Fig 1.113 Two trees by Mamselle. **a.** Tailored and elegant, this deeply textured, five-tier tree has only one rhinestone, and that is in its top star. 2.25" **b.** This tree looks a little like Trifari Fig 1.152c, but it is constructed with only one layer and has small baguette candles. 2.0" $40-65 each

Mexico.
Fig 1.114 This tree marked *Mexico* also *Sterling 925*. It is a flat layer with scored branches and enamel dot ornaments. 2.12" $25-45

M.J.ENT. The initials stand for M. J. Enterprises, Cranston, Rhode Island, which is still in business.

Fig 1.115 Two pins side by side. The first is signed *M. J. ENT*; the second, identical except for colors, is unsigned, though it does have a plate on the back where the signature would have gone. Both are open, feathery, two-layered trees with baguette candles and rhinestone flames—twenty-five stones in all, including the top. 2.0" $60-130 each

Monet. Founded in the late 1930s and still in business, each year Monet issues new Christmas tree pins that are sold in many department stores. They are signed ©*Monet*. When they disappear after Christmas, they rise in value. Now in the same firm as Trifari and Marvella.

Fig 1.116 Four trees by Monet. **a.** A tiny, solid-textured tree decorated with nine multicolored cabochons. 1.62" **b.** This imaginative, open tree is made of ribbon-like loops. It originally sold in department stores in 1997 for $20. 2.12" **c.** A slender tree of four shaggy-bottomed tiers decorated with fifteen tiny rhinestones in colors often found on trees by ART. 2.0" **d.** Another recent Monet tree, a single zigzag of metal, top to bottom, trimmed with rows of graduated, clear rhinestones, creates a striking modern tree. 2.75" $15-35 each

Fig 1.117 Two trees signed *MV*. Consider the peace symbols at the tops of these two trees by MV: They must have been made in the mid- to late 1960s. Both are in brushed silver metal. **a.** A slightly asymmetrical tree, solid except around the three larger stones. 3.12" **b.** Made of thirteen angels with their arms folded; there are no stones on this tree. 2.5" $45-100 each

Fig 1.118 Stones are false prong-set in this unusual, flashy tree by MYLU. In addition to the five large irregular faux pearls, there are seven square stones with pointed tops. I also have seen this tree with chartreuse stones and opaque pink stones replacing the pearls. This tree is probably not for the petite. 2.75" $45-120

Mylu. Two sisters, Marge Borofsky and Lynn Gordon, who began by designing Christmas corsages. Mylu began working with designs in metal in the mid-1960s. In 1968 it became a division of Coro. In the early 1970s, the sisters and Mike Tancer left Coro to form Tancer II.

Fig 1.119 Three trees that show the MYLU flare for design. **a.** An interesting outline tree decorated with just one rhinestone in its star. 3.25" **b.** A futuristic, geometric tree is asymmetrical with stones embedded in star-shaped craters in the metal. 2.25" **c.** Pushing the definition of Christmas tree is this very modernistic assembly of cross-hatched pieces—two verticals and seven horizontals. Twenty-seven rhinestones are embedded as ornaments. 3.25" $25-85 each

Fig 1.120 Three by MYLU. **a.** Four tiers of delicate leafy branches are decorated with thirty-seven clear aurora borealis stones. 2.75" **b.** Notice the similarity to Corel Fig 1.33c. Five tiers zigzag at the bottom with large clear stones fitted in between the tiers. In this example there are pearls below the top tier. 2.62" **c.** Another bold statement from MYLU uses texture instead of rhinestones to dazzle us. 2.75" $35-85 each

Fig 1.121 Two by MYLU. **a.** Composed of thirteen delicately formed poinsettias open to the back, this simple but stunning tree is sometimes found with a rhinestone-bordered pot. In this example, the stones are only in the flower centers. 3.0" See Fig 3.4b for MYLU's similar treatment of matching poinsettia wreath. **b.** A tree of holly leaves and red rhinestone berries in an embossed pot. 2.75" $35-85 each

Fig 1.122 Three MYLU trees. **a.** Like fancy doilies wrapped around a clear cone, the tree sits on a beautiful, decorative stand. It is embellished with just fourteen rhinestones. 2.5" **b.** A stately tree with six stones in its center top, the central portion is cut to the back with half-circles, each centered with a clear aurora borealis stone. The tree wraps slightly to the back. 2.75" **c.** A latticework tree with stone settings at the intersections of the diamonds. This tree can be found with other colored rhinestones. 2.75" $20-55 each

Fig 1.123 Two more MYLU trees. **a.** Open tree, with twenty-one small rhinestones on droopy branches with finger-like projections, sits in a very large pot. 2.5" **b.** Seven red aurora borealis faceted beads hang loose between deeply scored, inverted fans on this four-tiered tree. 2.5" $25-80 each

Fig 1.124 Four MYLUs. **a.** Signed earrings. These could be worn with any of a number of MYLU tree pins, including **b** and **d** in this photo. The branches are cut to the trunk; the trees, each with eight rhinestones, dangle from clip-backs that are decorated with a star. 1.5" $10-25 **b.** Very much like Fig 1.119b but with fewer tiers and different colored stones. 2.37" **c.** The stones sit high above the branches of this tree, ten branches per side, which are cut clear to the trunk. There are red rhinestones and faux pearls. 1.75" **d.** Similar to **c**, but with a broader trunk and a star instead of a plain stone at the top. Aurora borealis rhinestones and pearls brighten this tree. 2.0" **b-d**: $20-45 each

Fig 1.125 a. Another treatment of a MYLU lattice tree, here with red stones at the vertices and five faceted, dangly beads at the bottom. 2.75" **b.** Swooping, concave triangle cut open in several places with nine blue faceted beads hanging across the bottom and a blue stone at the top. Unfortunately, this striking MYLU example is losing some of its paint. 3.0" $35-80 each

Napier. This company started in Massachusetts in 1875 and is still in business in Connecticut, making this the country's oldest maker of fashion jewelry. The Napier name has been used since 1922.

Pakula. A Chicago-based company with manufacturing facilities in Providence, Rhode Island.

Fig 1.126 Four trees by Napier. **a.** A tailored tree of polished gold inverted *V*s, from each of which hangs a clear, pear-shaped stone. Simple, but elegant. 1.62" **b.** An open-outlined, slightly asymmetrical tree made of wire rope decorated with just seven tiny pearls. 2.0" **c.** A tiny, all-pewter tree deeply molded with knob ornaments and no rhinestones. 1.75" **d.** A fat triangle of prong-set rhinestones slightly open to the back in silver metal. 1.87" $20-55 each

Fig 1.127 Two trees by Pakula. Notice the similarity of each to trees by Hollycraft—the first is identical to Fig 1.76b and the second to Fig 1.77. **a.** Five tiers of double-rope drapes open to the back. Twenty-seven red and green stones. 2.5" **b.** The seven baguette candles on this tree have red enameled flames. In addition, there are seventeen red ornaments. 2.37" $25-65 each

Pearl, Erwin. A designer whose new Christmas trees are being made each year.

Fig 1.128 Two trees by Erwin Pearl. Both of these trees were purchased new in 1997 from a jewelry store in New York City. **a.** Colored ornaments appear to hang inside each branch of this asymmetric rhinestone outline tree. It sold new for $185. 2.37" **b.** A stunning abstract tree with clusters of clear rhinestones along the edges of the deeply textured gold pin. It sold new for $185. 2.25" $145-185 each

Fig 1.129 Two more trees by Erwin Pearl. Both are four-tier, gold-plated trees. Notice the similarity to the Hattie Carnegie Fig 1.28a. **a.** This tree was a new design in 1996. Twenty-seven tiny sliver balls hang freely from loops, one loop per branch. It sold new for $135. 2.12" **b.** Similar to the first, but slightly smaller, with red metallic balls. It sold new in 1997 for $175. 2.0" $135-175 each

Pell. 1941–present, run today by the youngest of the four brothers (none of them named Pell) who started the company.

Fig 1.130 Three green, red, and clear rhinestone candle trees by Pell, all solid surface. All candles are clear with red rhinestone flames and all tops are clear tears. **a.** Four branch end candles and nine large ornaments over a field of pavé green rhinestones—fifty-six stones in all on this 1.87" tree with serpentine bottom. **b.** Very similar to **a**, but much larger and with sharper branch definition. Same number of candles and ornaments, but with eighty-eight stones in all. 2.5" **c.** This tree has ten candles and a border of red all around the perimeter. Notice that the bottom is not serpentine but slightly convex. It has sixty-five stones and a simpler trunk than the other two pins in this figure. 2.0" $55-95 each

Fig 1.131 Three trees by Pell. All have vertical garlands, similar tiers of branches, each cut back to the trunk, and straight metal trunks. All have small colored rhinestone ornaments embedded deeply in their branches. **a.** Nine tiers and three vertical streamer garlands of baguette rhinestones on this symmetrical tree. 2.5" **b.** The same nine-tiered structure but with a large star and a navette stone on top. Here, with five twisted silver wire garlands. 2.62" **c.** Two candles and five gold wire garlands on this smaller, seven-tiered tree. 2.5" $40-85 each

Fig 1.132 Three trees in red and green by Pell. The first and third have similar trunks, tops, and garlands. Each has baguettes on the trunk and a single stone top and diagonal garlands of red and green baguettes. **a.** This tree has a broad outline form and a few scattered green rhinestone ornaments in its open center. The ornaments embedded in the outline are all red. 2.25" **b.** A lovely open tree with pavé rhinestones set on crisscrossing garlands. There are four candles on branch ends and a row of eight large ornaments across the bottom. Compare this to Fig 1.333b. 2.62" **c.** A solid tree, mostly pavé green background with ten large, red ornaments. There are sixty-one stones in all. 2.12" $40-95 each

Fig 1.133 Three trees by Pell. **a.** Five skirt-like deep layers cut nearly to the trunk, each decorated with deeply embedded red, green, and blue ornaments. The bottom three layers have embedded baguette garlands. 2.5" **b.** Identical in form to Fig 1.132b, this tree is signed both *Pell* and *MBB* (for Mary Beth Bouchard). It differs only in the use of pearls in the trunk and on the garlands and the purple stones. The tear at the top is aurora borealis. 2.5" **c.** Similar in form but smaller than Fig 1.130b. It was purchased from a tuxedo jacket full of old Christmas pins for sale. The pavé stones are green and clear; it is decorated with four candles with orange rhinestone flames and nine larger ornaments. 2.5" $45-110 each

Robert. Began to use the signature "Originals by Robert" in 1960 and continued to do so until the late 1970s.

Fig 1.135 These two trees by Robert both have green foliage. **a.** Here, individual leaves all grow from a central point at the base. Prong-set rhinestones and hanging pearls decorate this lovely tree. 2.62" **b.** Identical to Fig 1.155a, this tree has no prong-set stones and all of the beads are iridescent, faceted in red, green, and clear. 2.37" $110-175 each

Fig 1.134 Each of the pins in these three pictures are signed *Original by Robert* in what looks like an artist's pallet. All are planted in pots. The trees in this picture have translucent, unfaceted glass beads. **a.** A tiny, nugget-like tree with four vertical ridges and small red and green rhinestones glued into crevices, as well as eight red and green beads. 2.37" $110-175 **b.** Shiny, green foliage with both tiny red prong-set stones and hanging red beads. 1.75" $55-125 **c.** In this two-layer tree, the back layer is enameled white, the front is green. All of the stones except for the top clear rhinestone hang. To see a partridge in this tree, go to Fig 6.21a. 2.62" $70-150

Fig 1.136 Three more trees by Robert, this time without dangles. **a.** A small tree, much like a simple MYLU, in a rounded pot. Seventeen red and green rhinestone ornaments and one clear one in the top are glued in. 2.12" **b.** A very open tree, this is actually the back layer of the tree in Fig 1.134c. Here, it has four tiers of branches and fourteen multicolored glued-in stones. 2.62" **c.** A double-layered tree of branches very similar to the second tree. This tree is decorated with glued rhinestones and thirteen red or green baguette candles. This unusual tree is a barrette for holding back hair. 3.0" $110-175 each

St. John.

Fig 1.137 Simple and tailored, ten curved bars of this tree by St. John are held together by star and ornament settings. 2.5" $110- 140

St. Labre.

Fig 1.138 Two trees by St. Labre. **a.** The seven branches per side are completely covered in stones in multi-pronged settings. The three fan-like decorations hang free. There are four magenta ornaments and four clear baguette candles, each with amber rhinestone flames. Notice the unusual trunk with some red enameling and the enameled points to the top star. 2.62" $95-150 **b.** A solid, deeply textured tree with the uppermost areas of the branches frosted white. Notice the two packages and the greens at the bottom of the tree. This example is decorated with seventeen cabochon stones including the aqua green stone at the top, but I have also seen it with faceted red and green stones. 2.5" $65-160

Sandor. Founded around 1940, Sandor was an early producer of enameled costume jewelry. The Sandor name stood for quality. It ceased production in the mid-1970s.

Fig 1.139 Two trees signed Sandor. **a.** An enameled evergreen sits on a stand made of three square, faceted stones. The seven red and green ornaments are prong-set at a level high above the plane of the tree itself. 2.37" $20-50 **b.** Sandor has not made costume jewelry since about 1970, but this pin is currently being made using the Sandor signature. It sells as a new tree at the Brimfield antique show for about $30-40. The paint quality is not good. 3.0" Buyer beware!

Swarovski. This manufacturer offers two lines of Christmas jewelry: The Jeweler's collection has been offered through department stores since about 1980, and the newer Signature collection has been available in boutiques since 1994. They have identical signatures: a swan in an oval.

Fig 1.140 This was the 1995 limited edition tree by Swarovski, sold only by Nordstrom. It is a truly breathtaking combination of long, faceted navettes, clear pavé rhinestones, and cabochon ornaments. It originally sold for $115; now it is nearly impossible to find. I was told that this edition was limited to 821 trees. 2.75" $450+

Fig 1.141 Three by Swarovski. **a.** This 1996 Swarovski limited edition tree for Nordstrom is slightly see-through with large, star-shaped rhinestones and other gold bordered stars of pavé rhinestones. It originally sold for $125. 2.5" $175+ **b.** This is a smaller tree from Swarovski's middle-priced Signature line. It is nearly covered with pavé rhinestones except for what look like shooting stars that end in small cabochon stones. It cost $70 new in 1996. 1.87" $70+ **c.** This one is also covered in clear stones, many of which are pavé; the rest are slightly skewed navettes encircled by a gold rim. It sold new in 1996 for $125. 2.5" $125+

Fig 1.142 Notice the beautiful enameling applied to the backs of the three Swarovski trees in Fig 1.141. In the center, smaller pin you can also see the swan which is the Swarovski signature used on both the Jeweler's and Signatures collections.

Fig 1.143 Nordstrom's 1997 limited edition Swarovski pin sold for $135. It is a very large, slightly asymmetrical tree cut by ribbons of gold with fields of clear pavé rhinestones, decorated with multi-colored, multi-shaped, faceted ornaments. It's a knockout. 2.75" $175+

Swoboda.

Fig 1.144 These three trees were photographed together because of their similarities. The first and third are unsigned, but because their pots look alike they may have been made by the same company. **a.** An open tree with jade leaves. The flowers are red glass cabochons. 1.75" **b.** The signature is difficult to read but looks like *Swoboda Inc*. It is a very open, flat tree with odd-sized, round stones that may be semi-precious glued to it. 1.5" **c.** This unsigned pin has uncut amethysts nearly covering the tree, creating a broad-leaf effect. 1.87" $40-100 each

Tancer II. Another offshoot of Coro, it was begun in the mid-70s by Michael Tancer and the two sisters who had founded MYLU. Tancer II stands for *Tancer and two.*

Fig 1.145 Three trees by Tancer II. Because Tancer II evolved from MYLU, it is no surprise that we see innovative, wonderful trees with this signature. **a.** Here is a whimsical, modernistic design of three sections bordered in rope with star-shaped settings. There are two large, watermelon tourmaline stars, one at the top and one that dangles from the bottom tier. 2.87" $45-100 **b.** This is a large, open-frame, four-tier tree. From it hang ten flat, navette-shaped stones, each in its own gold frame. Enameled panels at the side and base pick up the same colors. A red cabochon decorates the star. 2.75" $45-100 **c.** A tree of vertical diamonds, most with a tiny knob in the center, a few with rhinestone ornament decorations. 2.25" $25-40

Fig 1.146 Five trees by Tancer II. **a.** A triangle-shaped tree cut into diamonds and decorated with raised flowers and aurora borealis rhinestones. Five faceted beads hang from the bottom. 2.75" **b.** This tree's most prominent features are its watermelon tourmaline star at the top and its broad trunk, in which some viewers see a face. It is decorated with just seven tiny additional rhinestones. 2.12" **c.** A classic MYLU design—some branches forward, thirteen to a side. Notice how the roots curl up at the bottom of the trunk. This example is decorated with red, green, and clear aurora borealis stones. 2.5" **d.** A silver tree with thirteen pink poinsettias, some with pink knobs for centers. Five have green stones. 2.5" **e.** Five green navettes and five clear rhinestones decorate this open-branched, gold tree. 2.12" $15-45 each

Fig 1.147 Two trees featuring the Mack Truck bulldog. A Mack Truck employee told me that these trees were sold at the employee novelty shop. **a.** Signed *Tancer II*, it looks like Fig 1.146c, except for metal and stone color—and the bulldog prominently hanging from it. 2.5" **b.** The bulldog is superimposed on top of this unsigned tree of lovely, dark metal; it has a richly detailed pot. There are thirty-four tiny simulated pearls and multicolored stones. 2.25" $40-80 each

Fig 1.148 More Tancer II. **a.** A very open, slender triangle made of star outlines and adorned with twenty red, green, and clear aurora borealis stones, mostly between the stars. 3.0" **b.** There was no question whether or not this tree was politically correct in the 1970s, when it was made. Its fur center probably attracted as much attention then as it does now. Notice that here the curved wire often seen on the base of MYLU and Tancer II trees is used very handsomely all the way around to create a border. Just one clear aurora borealis stone at the top. 2.5" $30-60 each

Fig 1.149 Four Tancer II trees. **a.** See Fig 1.146b. **b.** A familiar Tancer and MYLU design, here in silver and with an atypical straight trunk bottom. Seventeen blue and green rhinestones. 2.5" **c.** Identical to the MYLU doily tree Fig 1.122a, except here in a lighter, brighter gold. Ten red and green stones and some clear aurora borealis stones. 2.5" **d.** In pale gold, this is a broad outline tree with three inverted fans down the center, open between the fans. Red and green rhinestones are set deep in the middle, and there is a clear aurora borealis at the top—thirteen stones in all. 2.25" $20-40 each

Torino.

Fig 1.150 Two trees by Torino. **a.** This green-enameled tree was made in two layers. The top layer has two additional vertical projections, so it looks like a three-layer tree. Ornaments are all located at the tips of the branches, thirteen in all including the top star. 2.25" **b.** An open, dark brass tree of inverted fans of pine needles, each held in place by a rhinestone. A few rhinestones are set between the fans at the bottom of the tree, also. Unusual purple and orange rhinestones are included in the total of twenty. 2.0" $35-65 each

Tortolani. 1960–1975.

Fig 1.151 This is an unusual design in pewter by Tortolani. The trunk of the tree is a long candle with the flame as the top; the stand is the base. This tree stands by itself. One-half of the tree has swooping branches, the other half pine needles, cones, a star and a bell. Fourteen red and green rhinestones. 2.5" $40-70

Trifari. Fashion designer of fine jewelry from 1918–present. They made Christmas jewelry beginning in the 1950s.

Fig 1.152 Three trees by Trifari. **a.** A lovely tree of vertical gold slats crisscrossed by raised beaded garlands. Slightly open to the back, it is decorated with eleven pink rhinestones and a clear rhinestone in the star top. 2.25" **b.** This tree has a different Trifari signature, script rather than the usual block lettering. It is also the only Trifari tree pictured that does not have a trunk with roots. This is a tiny, solid tree with simple braid garland, thirteen red ornaments, and a clear stone in the top star. 1.87" **c.** In this two-layer tree of brushed gold, each branch has a raised border of polished gold. This tree was also made with no stones. Here, it has a clear rhinestone top and twelve colored ornaments set in false-prong settings. 2.0" $25-80 each

Fig 1.153 These three trees by Trifari are identical except for the color of the stones. The settings are slightly open to the back between jelly-like, translucent molded glass. Between these translucent settings are tiny rhinestones. Each tree has eighteen jelly stones and twenty tiny rhinestones. 2.12" each. **a.** Tiny stones are green. **b.** In this multicolored tree, the tiny stones are clear. **c.** The tiny stones are red. $105-220 each

Vendome. A division of Coro remembered for its high quality jewelry, 1944–1979.

Fig 1.154 This tree by Vendome has two layers, and the flower pot base is another layer yet of gold wire wrapped around a grooved frame. The grooves hold the wires much as would a stringed instrument. Flat-backed rhinestones are glued directly to the frame and the single rhinestone in the multi-pointed star is also glued in—fourteen stones in all. 2.37" $60-110

Vrba, Larry. Larry Vrba was the head designer for Miriam Haskell from 1970–1978. He also designed for Castlecliff, Les Bernard, the Metropolitan Opera, and the New York theater. His designs have been featured in *Women's Wear Daily*. He is currently designing Christmas jewelry.

Fig 1.155 Larry Vrba trees are not for the timid. They combine bold design, large size, and unusual color to make a statement. In this example, the stones completely cover the metal. Most are prong-set; some are glued. There are six candles with clear flames and a lovely flower-like top. 4.0" $150-225

Fig 1.156 In this Larry Vrba example, many branch-like arms of the tree are curved forward to create three dimensions. In addition, some candles are boldly extended on wire toward the viewer. There are nine candles in all. All the stones except those in the base and star top are prong-set. 4.0" $150-225

Fig 1.157 An elegant Larry Vrba all-white tree made of flower forms, thirteen in all, slightly open to the back. There is a square stone set in the top star. All stones are prong-set. 3.87" $120-185

Fig 1.158 This Larry Vrba tree seems to take its inspiration from the Weiss six-candle tree Fig 1.161a. The colors are bolder, however, and at 3.62" it is considerably larger. $150-225

Warner. Founded and run by Joseph Warner during the middle decades of the 20th century.

Fig 1.159 a. The stones completely cover this lovely tree by Warner. It must have inspired a similar tree by Eisenberg in 1992 Fig 1.46a. All the stones are prong-set, and there are four baguette candles with flames, two without. The tree is slightly convex in the center. 2.5" $60-135 **b.** Unsigned earrings, but in design and colors that match the Warner trees. There are clear baguette centers and deep rose stones at each end, all prong-set. 1.12" $25-45 **c.** Similar in many ways to the first tree, but a four-candle version. The lower candles have rhinestone flames. 2.0" $50-110

Fig 1.160 More by Warner. All of these have very delicate-looking tops, vertical gold streamers in two layers, decorated with tiny, prong-set rhinestones. Each piece has a tear drop top and prong-set, baguette candles with rhinestone flames. **a.** Dangle earrings, unsigned, but obviously made to match either of these trees. They consist of just the top half of either, open at the bottom and to the back. All stones are prong-set. The dangle alone measures 1.5." $80-110 **b.** Below this unusual tree with its solid, flat bottom are four enameled packages and a stand. This tree can be found both signed and unsigned. 2.12" $80-140 **c.** This tree is sometimes called the "chandelier tree." There is no metal base; instead, vertical wires are strung from the base of the tree to the rim, and horizontal drapes of tiny prong-set rhinestones wrap it. 2.37" $80-135

Weiss. Founded in 1942 by a former Coro employee, it continued in production until the early 1970s. Some of their creations were original with them, some bought from others. This signature is being used again and the jewelry does not compare favorably to the old Weiss.

Fig 1.161 Although there are candles on other Weiss trees, these are the three famous Weiss "candle trees." They are identified by the number of candles—six, five, or three. The six-candle Weiss seems to be the most desirable, though the three-candle is much more difficult to find.* All three trees are set in a brassy, gold-colored metal and beautiful, prong-set stones, but the smallest can be found with glued-in stones. The color combination used on this tree account for much of its desirability. I have seen the largest tree with a japanned back, though this is unusual. **a.** 2.75" $120-180 **b.** 2.12" $60-150 **c.** 1.87" $60-120

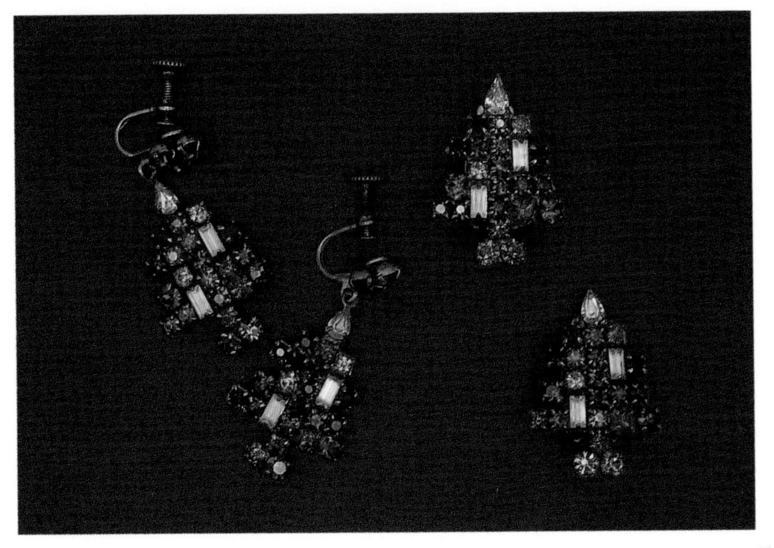

Fig 1.162 Two pairs of earrings that match the candle trees. Although the first pair is not signed, the trees are identical in color and appearance to the back of the second pair. **a.** These hanging earrings are much more difficult to find. The tiny 1.25" tree hangs from a screwback decorated with three rhinestones. $145-195 **b.** The back of the clip on these clip-on earrings is signed *Weiss*. 1.25" $75-130

* This pin is being reproduced.

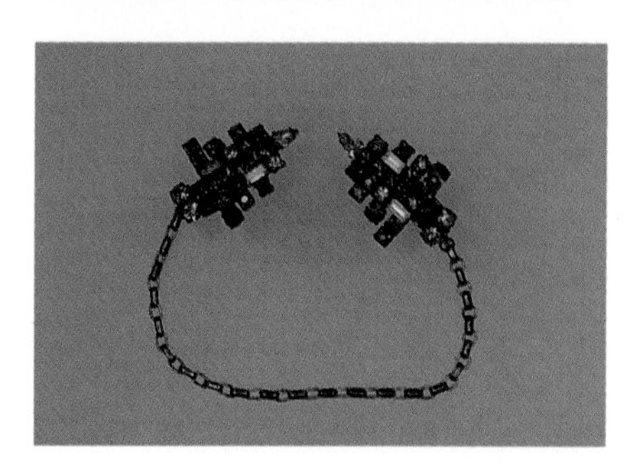

Fig 1.163 This is the sweater guard made like the Weiss earrings. Here, the tiny tree is attached to an alligator clip. Sweater guards were popular in the 1950s to keep a sweater from falling off when it was draped around your shoulders. This was bought on its original Albert Weiss card. I also have seen cufflinks made of these tiny trees. Each tree is 1.25" $175+

Fig 1.164 These two are sometimes called the "Victorian" Weiss trees. Each is of a dark brass, deeply scored. **a.** This is an almost two-layer tree with three mother-of-pearl baguette candles and amber rhinestone flames. The decorative ornaments are an unusual combination of primary colors, soft pastels, and a few deep-colored aurora borealis stones. This tree has a typical wide mound base. 2.5" **b.** Many of the same colored stones decorate this tree. Some are set deep in the branches; others are positioned high above them. The four candles are enameled; their flames are amber rhinestones. This is an atypical base for a Weiss tree. 2.37" $85-165 each

Fig 1.165 a. This angular tree has another common Weiss base, shaped like a slash or an arc. The tree is crossed by four raised braided garlands and cut to the back with S-shaped scrolls. The stones on these trees and earrings are glued in place. Some of them are iridescent. 2.5" $45-85 **b.** Clip-back earrings measure 1.0" $30-55 **c.** The much brighter small gold tree measures 2.0" $35-60

Fig 1.166 a. Matching the tree, each prong-set earring has three scalloped stones. Just 1.0" tall. $45-85 **b.** Bright brass Weiss much like Fig 1.165a, but much more tightly wrapped toward the back. The larger stones are prong-set and have tiny brass decorations on the tops. They look as if they were actually strung to the tree. There are two watermelon tourmalines and ten of its fourteen stones are scalloped. 2.5" $65-115

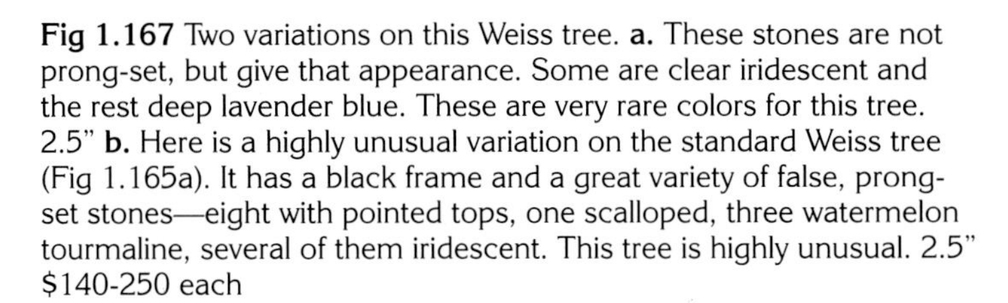

Fig 1.167 Two variations on this Weiss tree. **a.** These stones are not prong-set, but give that appearance. Some are clear iridescent and the rest deep lavender blue. These are very rare colors for this tree. 2.5" **b.** Here is a highly unusual variation on the standard Weiss tree (Fig 1.165a). It has a black frame and a great variety of false, prong-set stones—eight with pointed tops, one scalloped, three watermelon tourmaline, several of them iridescent. This tree is highly unusual. 2.5" $140-250 each

Fig 1.168 This Weiss tree is a large triangular field of flat-topped rhinestones in a border of shaggy brass needles. Wrapping slightly to the back, it is simple and stunning. 2.37" $140-225 (This same tree is found signed Hollycraft)

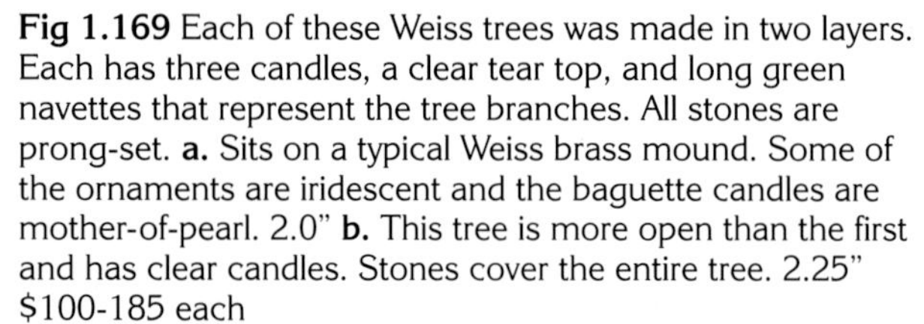

Fig 1.169 Each of these Weiss trees was made in two layers. Each has three candles, a clear tear top, and long green navettes that represent the tree branches. All stones are prong-set. **a.** Sits on a typical Weiss brass mound. Some of the ornaments are iridescent and the baguette candles are mother-of-pearl. 2.0" **b.** This tree is more open than the first and has clear candles. Stones cover the entire tree. 2.25" $100-185 each

Fig 1.170 A lovely delicate brushed gold Weiss pin with six textured, scalloped-bottom tiers, each with a row of tiny, clear rhinestones—I counted seventy-seven in all. 1.75" $55-130

Fig 1.172 Earrings and pin by Weiss. Notice the similarity between this set and the Warner set in Fig 1.159. However, this tree and earrings have glued-in stones and the colors are slightly different. The tree is less convex and it is more open to the back. **b.** Clip-back earrings have glued-in stones with a single candle in the center. Signed *Weiss* on the tree part. 0.87" $30-50 **b.** Six candles, four with amber-colored flames. The trunk has two round stones instead of the baguette found in the Warner. Signed *Weiss*. 2.37" $95-155

Fig 1.171 An elegant, open, lacy Weiss tree that has three tiers of very glittery dark green and dark red rhinestones. It has a clear stone in the star at the top. Look for its matching wreath in Fig 4.3. 2.75" $85-175

Fig 1.173 This lovely, enameled green tree is cut by four diagonal swags of clear rhinestones and sits on the classic Weiss mound. This is one of the easier Weiss trees to find. 2.62" $85-125

Fig 1.174 White enamel over feathery gold branches highlighted by iridescent stones makes for a winning combination for this Weiss tree. The tree rises from a flat decorated pot. *Weiss* is stamped directly into the metal. An unsigned version of this tree is not as carefully molded, but it is also very pretty. 2.37" $65-110

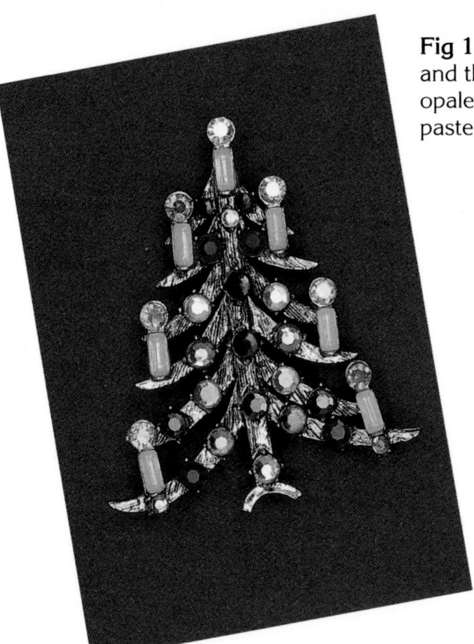

Fig 1.175 The structure of this tree is certainly not its strong point and the base is not at all typical of Weiss. But the large, unfaceted, opalescent candles with their iridescent flames are sensational. The pastel stones soften the bright, shiny gold. 2.75" $125-190

Fig 1.176 Three by Weiss. **a.** This tree is slightly open and has many small tongue-like projections with jagged bottoms. It has a soft wash of green and is decorated with ten large stones with eleven small amber stones between them. 2.37" **b.** Light green lace bedecked with nine large cabochons with fourteen tiny amber stones between them. It has the Weiss slash bottom and a teardrop top. 2.5" **c.** Tongue-like projections similar to the first tree, but they are easier to see because this tree is decorated with fewer and smaller red and green rhinestones—just sixteen including the top. It sits on the classic Weiss mound. 2.5" $65-135 each

Fig 1.177 Two trees by Weiss are identical except for coloration. Both have tear-shaped tops and slash bottoms. Both are solid except where slightly cut by six beaded garlands. Both have round and navette stones embedded in the flat areas as ornaments. 2.5" each. **a.** Enameled green. **b.** Unenameled. $50-110 each

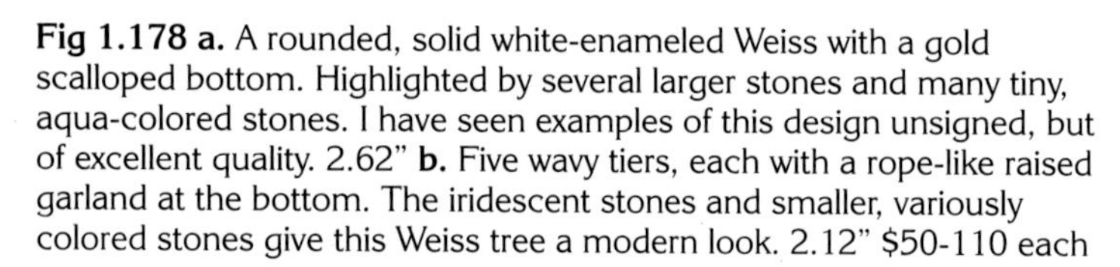

Fig 1.178 a. A rounded, solid white-enameled Weiss with a gold scalloped bottom. Highlighted by several larger stones and many tiny, aqua-colored stones. I have seen examples of this design unsigned, but of excellent quality. 2.62" **b.** Five wavy tiers, each with a rope-like raised garland at the bottom. The iridescent stones and smaller, variously colored stones give this Weiss tree a modern look. 2.12" $50-110 each

Fig 1.179 These Weiss trees would make nice daughter-and-mother pins. **a.** The smaller has two textured scalloped tiers decorated with stones in three different shapes. 1.62" **b.** The top two tiers are the same, but the bottom tier adds substantially to the overall size of this tree. 2.0" $50-100 each

Fig 1.180 These Weiss earrings were purchased on their original card. Ah, but are they trees? They are when they are kept in someone's Christmas tree collection! They dangle, and the stones at the bottom dangle from the dangles. The prong-set stones are beautiful colors of violet, magenta, and orange. 3.0" $75-125

Fig 1.181 Though signed *Weiss*, the jewelry shown here has given collectors some reason to believe that it is not old. This set very much resembles the Weiss six-candle tree set, and the backs are not plated. Although the pastel iridescent candles are particularly lovely, the green stones lack the interest and beauty of the much-sought Weiss six-candle tree. **a.** Each earring looks unfinished on the back, and the silver clip-back is attached to the brass fastener that protrudes from the tree. 1.5" **b.** The tree itself is slightly smaller than the true six-candle Weiss. I've seen a similar clear tree with a clear rhinestone background and pastel candles that has the same suspicious features. 2.5" $225 the set (but, is it worth it?)

New or Suspicious Weiss Pieces

Fig 1.182 While signed *Weiss*, this tree is suspect for the bright silver plating and its use of rhinestone chain that was soldered together. It is, however, a lovely tree and an unusual design. All the stones are clear, except eighteen green and twenty red. 2.67" $85-135

Fig 1.183 Two more pins that have the name *Weiss* incised into the back. These two trees were sold as new, not the old Weiss, at Brimfield, where they went for less than $50 each. Both of these trees are large and bold; neither is a design that I can be sure was made when Weiss was active in business, but both are well-made. **a.** Square prong-set stones ride above vertical, rope-like garlands on this open tree. The half-moon cabochon base is an unusual touch. 2.62" **b.** A slightly ridged tree with deep-cut branches that are ribbed at the top over vertical scoring. The candles are clear, slightly rounded rhinestones that are not foil-backed. The rest of the stones are red and green cabochons. 3.0" $40-70 each

Fig 1.184 These two Weiss trees, though very pretty, are acknowledged as new in the New York City area, where they are widely distributed. Both are flat, have applied oval cartouche signatures with *Weiss* in capital block letters curved over a ©. Both are made of soldered rhinestone chain and both have loose garlands of clear stones. **a.** This is sometimes found in other bright or darker colors. I have recently heard about this pin with a *KJL* mark on it. 2.25" **b.** I have only seen this size in the pastels. 1.87" $30-55 each

Fig 1.185 This tree was bought new during the Christmas season of 1997 at the J. B. White department store. It is signed *Weiss* on the back in a cartouche. It is on a Laura Gayle card, which is how it was purchased. It is a very pretty tree and sold new for $18. The faux pearls are false prong-set. 2.37" $18

Yoska. Gerard Yoska is a contemporary jewelry designer in New York City who specializes in editions limited to a very few hundred. He has not made any Christmas trees for the last several years.

Fig 1.186 A statement in design, this unconventional tree by Yoska is beautifully enameled. It was issued in 1987. 2.37" $125-175

Chapter 2

Unsigned Trees

Fig 2.2 An unusual older tree with a pewter-like finish. The base and trunk are a large candle. The three tiers have vertical cuts open to the back. Sixteen small rhinestones decorate the candle and tier bottom. 2.5" $45-95

Fig 2.1 A wonderful find! A tree in its original gift box, which is also a mailer. After the card on the inside was signed, the top of the box could be addressed and stamped. The paper covering the box top folds down and glues to the bottom. The instructions advise to "pull out and moisten glue flap for mailing." The mailer was designed by the Betsy Ross company of Paoli, Pennsylvania. It has no zip code, dating it to before 1964. The tree itself is pretty, but not unusual. Often found in pale gold, it is made of inverted fans and decorated with tiny knobs and forty-two deeply set rhinestones. 2.37" $35-95

Fig 2.3 Four unsigned trees in a light gold finish. **a.** This is reminiscent of the DeNicola tree Fig 1.38 but with the suggestion of raised branches in the front. It has forty-three rhinestones including those in the pot. 2.0" **b.** Though unsigned, this tree is identical in form to MYLU Fig 1.125b. 2.63" **c.** Five tiers, each made of irregular cut-out patches brushed with silver and decorated with a single, small stone—fourteen in all. 2.87" **d.** Somewhat similar to **a**, it has six fat tiers with textured branches and a single row of clear stones down the center. 2.0" $20-40 each

Fig 2.4 a. An open silver tree whose ropy blue branches are decorated with blue rhinestones. This tree was purchased new prior to 1962. 2.5" **b.** An older copy of the Hollycraft tree Fig 1.73c, this tree has only red ornaments and no baguette candles. 2.12" **c.** A silver triangular frame of sixteen stars that barely touch, there is a blue-gray rhinestone in the center of each star and one in the top. 2.12" **d.** I have seen this tree in brass and silver and with other rhinestone colors, but always with just one color (with the exception of the top stone) on each tree. I have been told that this example was purchased new in the 1950s. 2.75" **e.** Feathery, drooping branches hang from this tree, adorned with red stones. It is a little like Weiss Fig 1.174. 2.25" $20-40 each

Fig 2.5 Three green trees. **a.** Bright green streamers on this light gold tree display an assortment of rhinestone colors. 2.37" **b.** Dark green with some frosted white, this one is slightly open between the four tiers and has twenty-six rhinestones between red knobs along garlands at the bottom of each tier. 1.87" **c.** This slender, tall, three-tier tree looks very modern. It has a rhinestone top plus eight additional rhinestones, some of which extend from the tree edges. 2.75" $25-45 each

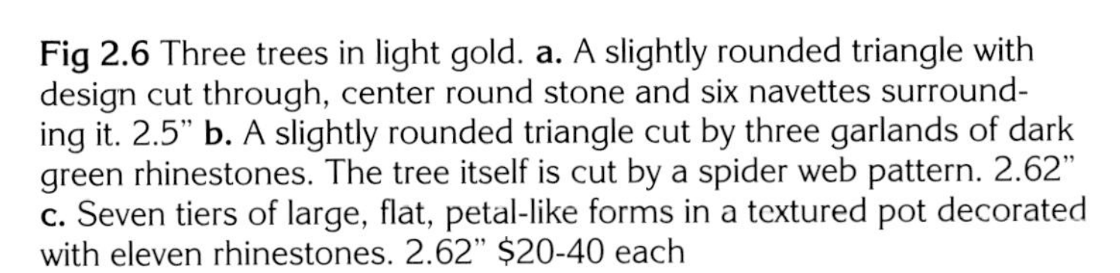

Fig 2.6 Three trees in light gold. **a.** A slightly rounded triangle with design cut through, center round stone and six navettes surrounding it. 2.5" **b.** A slightly rounded triangle cut by three garlands of dark green rhinestones. The tree itself is cut by a spider web pattern. 2.62" **c.** Seven tiers of large, flat, petal-like forms in a textured pot decorated with eleven rhinestones. 2.62" $20-40 each

Fig 2.7 It is difficult to know why someone would go to the trouble of making such a beautifully detailed tree and not put a name on it. This tree is composed of bunches of pine needles with a ribbon running through them. There are three bells hanging from the ribbon and seven candles, each with a tiny red flame. Each bell clapper has a rhinestone decoration, and there are rows of rhinestones around the bells. Altogether, a large, handsome tree carefully designed and crafted. 2.75" $35-80

Fig 2.9 Green navette trees. **a.** This is a slightly rounded tree with red stone trunk and decorations. Set in silver, the stones are an olive green; some are aurora borealis. 2.75" **b.** Whereas the branches in the first tree turn up, the branches in this one overlap going down. The pot resembles those used by Originals by Robert. Four tiers of navettes with red ornament decorations below some of them. 3.0" $60-125 each

Fig 2.8 Two simple designs composed mostly of dark green navettes. **a.** An open tree with navette branches and colored ornaments at the ends. A red navette forms the base. There are twenty-nine stones in all. 2.87" **b.** An even simpler design completely formed from just twelve green navettes. 2.62" $30-85 each

Fig 2.10 a. Prong-set stones, mostly clear navettes with a red navette top, nearly cover this silver tree. There are thirty-six rhinestones in all. Some of the ornaments are fixed, ten dangle. 3.0" **b.** This slightly open, green navette tree is decorated with four red, dangly, faceted stones and two loose garlands of clear rhinestones. 2.5" $60-130 each

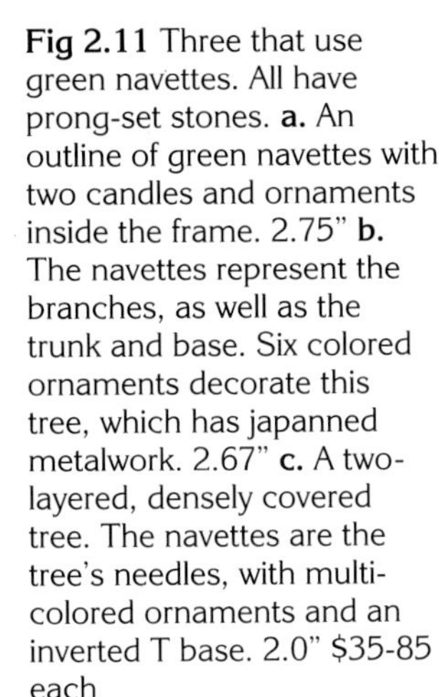

Fig 2.11 Three that use green navettes. All have prong-set stones. **a.** An outline of green navettes with two candles and ornaments inside the frame. 2.75" **b.** The navettes represent the branches, as well as the trunk and base. Six colored ornaments decorate this tree, which has japanned metalwork. 2.67" **c.** A two-layered, densely covered tree. The navettes are the tree's needles, with multi-colored ornaments and an inverted T base. 2.0" $35-85 each

Fig 2.12 This tree with its star top and four tiers of green navettes will stand upright on its circular base. Three faceted, red aurora borealis beads and two clear garlands decorate it. 2.5" $40-110

Fig 2.13 a. The green, unfaceted navette branches point up on this tree. The ornaments are aurora borealis. 2.5" **b.** This unusual asymmetrical design uses long, thin, faceted navettes and aurora borealis garlands. 2.25" **c.** Notice how much this gold-set tree looks like Napier Fig 1.126d, even to the color of the navettes. 2.0" $40-100 each

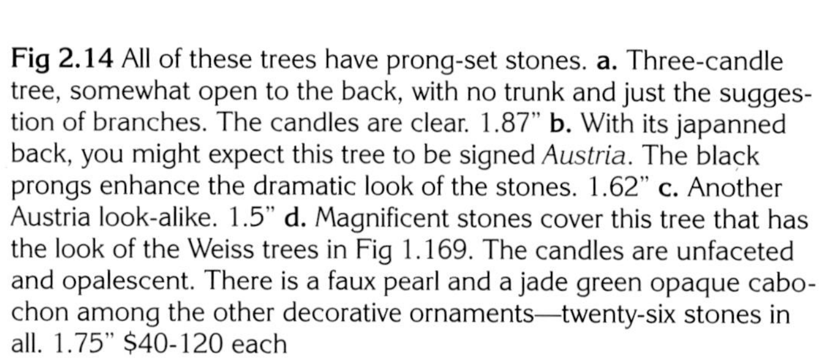

Fig 2.14 All of these trees have prong-set stones. **a.** Three-candle tree, somewhat open to the back, with no trunk and just the suggestion of branches. The candles are clear. 1.87" **b.** With its japanned back, you might expect this tree to be signed *Austria*. The black prongs enhance the dramatic look of the stones. 1.62" **c.** Another Austria look-alike. 1.5" **d.** Magnificent stones cover this tree that has the look of the Weiss trees in Fig 1.169. The candles are unfaceted and opalescent. There is a faux pearl and a jade green opaque cabochon among the other decorative ornaments—twenty-six stones in all. 1.75" $40-120 each

Fig 2.15 The earrings and first tree are a set of outline trees in pewter-like silver adorned with beautiful aurora borealis stones and silver knobs. **a.** Earrings 1.12" $20-35 **b.** Tree pin 2.37" $25-60 **c.** A triangle of web-like dark silver filigree decorated with knobs and aurora borealis stones evenly spaced about it. 2.75" $30-70

Fig 2.16 a. The tall triangle with lacey outside edges and a base of gnarly roots is slightly open to the back. I have seen this tree with stones in several color combinations. 2.5" **b.** Two-layered tree, quite unusual, with deep projections and vertical grooves. It has seven candles and an unusual arc base. 2.37" **c.** A triangle cut into small diamonds, each of which holds one small, pastel-colored rhinestone. 2.5" $25-65 each

Fig 2.17 a. This ivory-colored, four-tiered tree sits in a gold frame. The stones look very much like those used on ART trees. 2.25" **b.** This modest cameo-like tree is set in a light gold metal frame. Both the stars and the tree are raised above the surface of the olive green background. 1.62" **c.** Made in two layers, the outer rim of gold-plated metal and the inner of silver-plated metal, the interior of this tall triangle is cross-hatched. Inside each section is a glittery, clear rhinestone—thirty in all. 2.5" **d.** The pale gold frame of this tree supports flat, mother-of-pearl slabs—a very unusual effect. Thirteen red and green rhinestones add glitter. 2.12" **e.** This fur-clip becomes a tree when its owner decides that is what it is. Certainly, its colors, its baguette-centered trunk, and its shape make it appropriate for inclusion in a tree collection. 2.62" **a-d**: $25-65 each; **e**: $55-125

Fig 2.18 a. Flat, pewter, broadleaf plant in a large pot has seven colored baguette candles and four round ornaments. 2.5" **b.** Black-framed triangular lattice with one stone in each open area of the latticework. 2.67" **c.** A tall, thin, broad-leafed tree, frosted white, in a pot. It is flat and very open to the back. 2.5" $25-60 each

Fig 2.19 The first and third are variations on the same tree—the first has more stones and different coloration, but both are symmetrical, rounded triangles, slightly domed, and open to the back. Both are 2.5" **a.** Eighteen stones. **b.** This dress clip requires some imagination to see it as a tree. Its owner has that imagination. 2.5" **c.** Eleven stones. $20-55 each

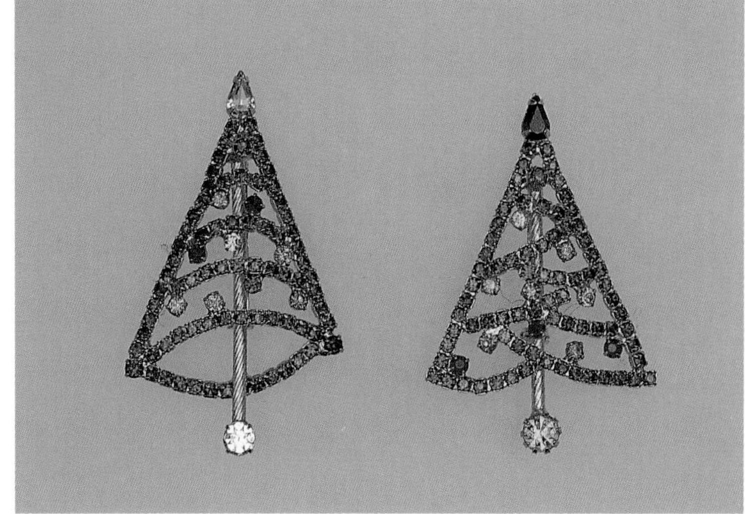

Fig 2.20. The stones are prong-set in these two unsigned trees, which look as if they were made by the same manufacturer. Each is a very open, triangular tree that uses the same colors of ornamental stones. **a.** Five horizontal curved garlands; the back portion of the bottom runs behind the trunk. 2.5" **b.** A triangle frame with crisscrossing garlands and ornaments between them. The trunk is twisted. 2.37" $40-60 each

Top left: **Fig 2.21 a.** Crisscrossing garlands separate areas of colored stone clusters on this broad triangle. 2.5" **b.** Four tiers of long, green loops open to the back confirm the endless innovation in Christmas tree design. Twelve red stones, including the top. 2.37" **c.** Stone colors are arranged to emphasize again and again the broad, triangular shape of this tree. 2.5" $30-60 each

Bottom left: **Fig 2.22 a.** Two similar layers of deeply cut, textured branches form this tree. It is decorated with fourteen multi-colored candles, each with its own red rhinestone flame. 2.37" **b.** A small tree of lovely and unusual colors. The branches are channel-set square stones and the clear ornaments are set along the trunk and at the ends of the branches. There are eighty-eight stones in all. This tree originally sold at Jordan Marsh, probably in the early 1960s. 2.12" **c.** This is a two-layer tree, the back layer flat and louvered, the front layer a rounded triangle with zigzag sides. The center is filled with small stone settings. In this case, the stones are pastels, but I have seen it with multi-colored stones and with very dark colored stones. It is lovely and not difficult to find. 2.5" $25-75 each

Top center: **Fig 2.23** These unsigned trees each consist of two layers of metal clipped together. Into the top layer, beads are threaded through holes. The back layer covers the bead wire and provides a place for the pin. See Fig 2.24. **a.** Approximately forty faceted beads, faux pearls, and tiny, colored stones are strung to the front plate of this pin. The rhinestones are prong-set. 2.0" **b.** Scallop-edged, sequined beads in pastel aurora borealis or iridescent colors are pinned to this smaller tree. 1.5" **c.** Here, the beads are all dark colors—deep lavender, watermelon tourmaline, and teal. 1.87" $30-50 each

Fig 2.24 Here you can see the inside of a tree shown in Fig 2.23. A single wire is threaded from one bead to the next. To finish the pin, the front and back are clipped together.

Fig 2.26 Two unsigned Hollycraft look-alikes. **a.** In white metal, this long, sinuous curve is decorated with clear aurora borealis stones. 2.25" **b.** Nearly identical to Hollycraft Fig 1.75. 2.37" $30-60 each

Fig 2.25 a. Prong-set clear rhinestones nearly cover this triangle. The base is a silver wire that curls back on itself. Seventy-eight rhinestones. 2.0" **b.** Stones are glued to this triangular tree. They are lovely, large, clear aurora borealis. 2.0" **c.** Prong-set rhinestones in fourteen flower-like formations cover this tree. 2.0" **d.** Seventeen rhinestone spheres are wired to this double-layer tree. The top stone of each sphere is a colored rhinestone—a very unusual tree. I counted roughly 187 stones. 2" $30-60 each

Fig 2.27 a. The enamel work on these leaves shows leaf veining and other attention to detail and is contained in a gold, zigzag border. The rounded cabochon-like stones are opaque and cherry-red. Notice the similarity to wreath Fig 3.4e. 2.0" **b.** Deep green-colored ropy metal forms the branches in this outline tree. It is slightly open to the back and there are sixteen colored rhinestone ornaments. 2.25" $25-50 each

Fig 2.29 Two tall unsigned trees, both rather modern-looking. **a.** Five tiers nearly solid in back, with eleven stones of several shapes, colors, and sizes. 3.37" **b.** A handsome, very slender, tall tree planted in a rhinestone decorated pot—a total of sixteen stones in all. The metal is scored from the center to each side, hinting at branches. 3.12" $20-45 each

Fig 2.28 a. Seven rope-like threads come together at the top of this modest tree, which is very open to the back and has garlands across the bottom. sixteen ornaments, one at the top and the rest on the ropes. 2.62" **b.** A very flat, stamped tree, this has feathery branches and a crown-like pot. Fourteen flat-backed stones are glued to the surface. The back says *HD357*. 2.5" **c.** This two-layer tree has green branches in back, gold in front—ten on each side. Sixteen ornaments rest between the front branches. 2.5" **d.** Stones decorate the star and pot of this tree. The basic element of the tree itself is a lacey sheet of metal, slightly bent in the center. 2.37" **e.** Stones alternate with knobs between the six diagonal swags on this open triangle tree. 2.62" **f.** This tree is a tall triangle of spider webs with rhinestones and gold knobs caught up in it and a large square faceted stone in the base— thirty-two stones in all. I've also seen this tree with stones in other color combinations. 2.75" $20-45 each

Fig 2.30 Two unsigned trees in white. **a.** An open, bare-branched tree highlighted with glittery white enamel. Just nine small rhinestones decorate this tree. 3.5" **b.** Prong-set stones, some open to the back, cover this tree. Most are opaque white, but the trunk and six small ornaments are clear aurora borealis stones. This tree is convex in the center. 3.25" $40-85 each

Fig 2.31 Four modestly priced, unsigned trees found in many variations on the East Coast. All have prong-set stones, and many have stones of unusual shapes, colors, or textures. **a.** A total of fifty-eight stones are set in horizontal rows in this tree of silver-colored metal. 2.25" **b.** Set in a gold metal, the clear and tan colored stones are cabochons. The others are faceted. Two round stones have broad, pink stripes in them. 2.25" **c.** The most unusual feature of this tree is its green navette base with a bumpy surface. It is set in silver and some of the stones are cabochon, some in settings open to the back. Above the green base are two small, coral-colored, opaque stones. 2.37" **d.** There are many unusual stones in this tree: the multifaceted, teardrop top, the two opalescent pink navettes midway down the tree, the lavender and green stones with the textured surface. 2.5" $20-70 each

Fig 2.32 An unsigned set in purple and clear aurora borealis stones. There are many versions of this style, which may have been produced over a long period of time. This is somewhat reminiscent of Weiss, Warner, and the 1992 Eisenberg pins. **a.** The tree, with six purple candles, is 2.25". $35-80 **b.** With a single purple candle, the clip-back earrings are 0.87". $15-35

Fig 2.33 a. Six dark green branches stretch up from either side of the twisted trunk of this silver tree. Fifteen ornaments, many of them dark-colored, are buried in the foliage. 2.12" **b.** To me, this tree looks like it is made of bananas. Notice the unusual red enamel pronged stand. Ten brilliant rhinestones are nested among the bananas. 2.25" **c.** An outline of two to three rows of green stones surrounds a center of four metal flower forms, each with its own rhinestone center—seventy-seven stones in all. 1.87" **d.** This two-layer tree is similar in construction to the BJ tree Fig 1.18b in that the back layer is foiled. Here, the front layer is crossed by horizontal garlands, and small, green stones hang from zigzag ropes along the garlands. There are twelve stones in all. 2.37" **e.** Each branch segment is a green holly leaf on this tree, which is open to the back and planted in a red pot. The metal is a light gold. 2.37" **f.** This tree has three clear baguette candles. It mimics the Weiss tree Fig 1.164a. 2.5" $20-45 each

Fig 2.34 Is it a Christmas tree? The owner says it is. It is a bare, deciduous, asymmetrical tree decorated with eleven clear, red and green prong-set ornaments. 2.0" $60-90

Fig 2.36 a. A tall, triangular frame with a serpentine bottom outlines the lacy inside of this open tree. It is decorated with just nine rhinestones, including the top. 3.12" **b.** Six tiers of winding rope, very open to the back, form this triangle. The red and green rhinestones course down the center and at the edges. 2.25" **c.** This tree is an open triangle cut by six wavy, flat ribbon garlands and decorated with eight red and green rhinestone ornaments. 2.0" **d.** A tree of vertical wires cut by three horizontal garlands. Each garland has its own bow, and a rhinestone is centered in each bow knot. There are ten rhinestones in all, including the top. 2.25" **e.** The front layer of this two-layer tree is bent forward slightly. This tree has a lovely, long trunk as well, and rhinestones embedded deeply in its surface. 2.37" $15-35 each

Fig 2.35 a. The black frame of this very delicate-looking tree enhances the drama of the dark-colored stones. Six slender, clear, baguette candles have amber rhinestone flames. 2.5" **b.** Prong-set stones cover this tree, which is made of loose rhinestone chain. The green triangle edges have been soldered, but the center rhinestones hang free. A large star of six clear rhinestones tops this very pretty tree. 2.5" **c.** This is a black metal tree, reminiscent of several Hollycraft trees except for its slash base. The large stones are set above double drapes, with clear rhinestones dotted between them. 2.5" $30-85 each

Fig 2.37 a. An open, feathery tree decorated with amethyst-colored, translucent stones that are natural-shaped—fourteen in all. 2.25" **b.** A solid frame around six free-form, slightly domed, translucent green glass shapes forms this most unusual tree. It has rows of clear rhinestones and a few colored rhinestones at its edges. I have not seen another tree like it. 2.12" **c.** A modern, fat, gold frame divides into five stained glass sections. Thirteen clear rhinestones decorate the trunk, the tree, and the star at the top. 2.0" $35-85 each

Fig 2.38 a. Stones nearly cover the branches of this wooden-looking little tree. Many of them, including the base, are baguettes. There are tiny green rhinestones around the red center in the star at the top. 2.12" **b.** Prong-set rhinestones completely cover this open tree. It has three branches per side and the amber garlands hang free. 2.37" **c.** A tiny, older tree of prong-set rhinestones. 1.87" $20-55 each

Opposite page bottom right: **Fig 2.39** At 4.25 inches, this tree is definitely for a taller person. The dangle in the center hangs free and the three sections of the triangle are each identical triangles themselves. Each stone sits in a double loop. This tree has a substantial base. $55-95

Fig 2.40 Three in white. **a.** A Hollycraft and Pakula look-alike—see Figs 1.77 and 1.127—this tree has enameled candles and flames. The rhinestones are all clear aurora borealis. The white enamel is gold-glittered. 2.25" **b.** Five separate tiers with jagged edges and heavy white frosting. 2.75" **c.** A seven-tier outline around an open field of clear rectangular stones set with open backs. 2.5" $15-50 each

Fig 2.41 All these are are made of bunches of green pine needles. **a.** This tree has a rhinestone decorated pot and soft-colored stones among its needles. 2.12" **b.** This tree has seven soft-colored baguette candles and flames and a few ornaments. It sits in a brown enamel pot. 2.0" **c.** This looks like the second tree, except that it is a bit taller, seven candles, and one side has been bent back. Was this a casting mistake? 2.12" $20-45 each

Fig 2.42 This unusual tree has tiers of aqua rhinestones, dark green at the bottom, interspersed with vertical aqua baguettes that have openings to the back between them. The stones are either set deep into the metal or the tree has been replated. Either way, the effect is lovely. 2.0" $60-125

Fig 2.43 Stones cover the metal on all five of these newer trees. **a.** A simple form with four swooping branches per side and alternating colors on the branches—a total of seventy-two rhinestones. 2.5" **b.** A tree primarily of green with some other colored stone decorations. 2.37" **c.** This tree has a rigid outside frame and five loose drapes running across it, rigid at the center. 2.5" **d.** This open tree has yellow navette candles. Its three bottom sections hang freely. 2.5" **e.** Similar to the previous tree but without the candles and the red tear at the top. 2.12" $20-30 each

Fig 2.44 All the trees here have prong-set stones. **a.** Here is a solid triangle with slightly jagged edges over a solid rhinestone pot. The tree is mostly green with a few colored ornaments scattered about and clear rhinestones along the edges. 2.37" **b.** A bit reminiscent of the Dorothy Bauer garland trees, this one is made of garlands, each containing two rows of rhinestones, one color per row. 2.5" **c.** Open to the back with a very tall trunk over its pot, this has five green branches per side with ornaments between them. 3.87" **d.** Green tree with rows of rhinestones in diagonal patterns, three loose garlands of clear rhinestones, and a few colored ornament stones. A very similar tree was offered by Eisenberg in 1996 for $40. 2.37" $20-55 each

Fig 2.45 a. A large, curved triangle of green and gold holly leaves and red berries that look much like those on many Weiss wreathes and boughs. It is slightly open to the back. There are no rhinestones. 2.37" **b.** There is a bright green wash on this light gold tree. It is nearly overwhelmed by its six large, colored baguette candles, equally spaced. 1.87" **c.** Here, green-washed branches are cut to the trunk, open to the back between. Ten multi-colored ornaments provide decoration. 2.0" **d.** A very broad tree of sections highlighted with white, open to the back. The thirteen stones scattered on the tree are mostly pastels. 1.75" $20-40 each

Fig 2.46 a. Open wire loops frame amber, magenta, and orange stones on this lacey-looking tree. There are twenty stones in all, most centered in loops. 2.37" **b.** The surface of this triangular tree is like the back layer of Fig 2.22c. It has the louvered look I described there. With no stones, it does have an angel sitting in its center. 2.25" **c.** This is a tiny tree of solid, textured gold, but in contains a pewter nativity insert that is open to the back. There are five clear rhinestones—four on the tree and one on the top. 1.5" **d.** A mate to Fig 2.45a, this is a topiary holly tree in a red pot with green and gold leaves and red berries—no rhinestones. The trunk is set off by a red bow. 2.5" $20-60 each

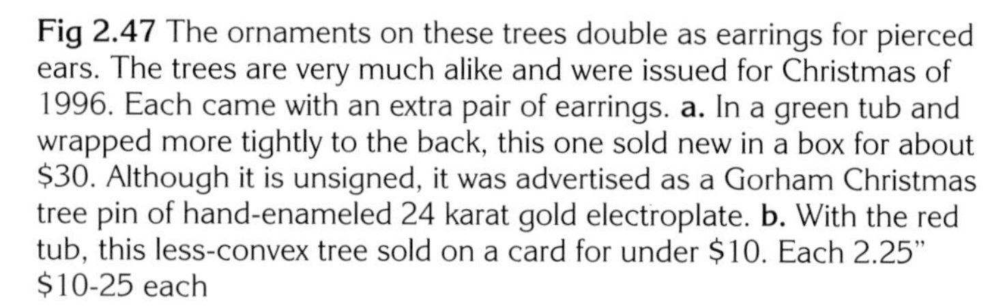

Fig 2.47 The ornaments on these trees double as earrings for pierced ears. The trees are very much alike and were issued for Christmas of 1996. Each came with an extra pair of earrings. **a.** In a green tub and wrapped more tightly to the back, this one sold new in a box for about $30. Although it is unsigned, it was advertised as a Gorham Christmas tree pin of hand-enameled 24 karat gold electroplate. **b.** With the red tub, this less-convex tree sold on a card for under $10. Each 2.25" $10-25 each

Fig 2.48 Three unsigned trees that copy other signed trees. The first two are copies of the Hollycraft garland tree. The last two were purchased in San Francisco for $5 each. **a.** This is an older copy with lovely crisscrossed garlands of aurora borealis rhinestones. The quality of the molding of this piece is not as good as Hollycraft, but the design and use of stones is lovely. 2.25" $25-55 **b.** Another copy, here in a bright gold. This tree is certainly a good value at $5, but you would not care to pay a Hollycraft price for it. 2.37" $10 or less **c.** A copy of the Eisenberg knob tree Fig 1.43a &d. There is even a plaque on the back where the Eisenberg signature would usually appear; this one is blank. The quality of the rhinestones is very good. 2.0" $10 or less

Fig 2.49 a. A brush tree, probably from the 1950s, on a wooden stand is actually half a tree with a red ribbon bow around the trunk. The branches are white-tipped. It has nine ornaments wired to the trunk and a paper tag that says *Japan*. 2.75" **b.** A red candy-cane with two composition, glittered bells. There are eighteen glass ornaments, including the two bell clappers. A paper ticket reads *Woolworth 10¢*. 5.0" $10 each

Chapter 3

Wreathes, greenery, and flowers

Fig 3.1 These Weiss wreathes have beautiful ribbon bows, holly leaves, and painted berries. **a.** This magnificent wreath comprises two layers riveted together. The back layer is a solid green and slightly larger; the front is gold with applied green enamel paint. 2.37"* **b.** A holly spray in two layers, the top considerably smaller than the bottom, with the bow placed in the center. 2.37" in its longest dimension. **c.** A bow is at the bottom of the small holly spray. Hanging free are two brass bells with little brass clappers that jingle softly. 2.5" $20-70 each

*This wreath has been reproduced.

Fig 3.2 Four wreaths by Weiss and one (in the center) unsigned. **a.** This holly wreath is constructed as a single mounded layer. It has leaves of pale and dark green and enameled berries scattered throughout. It is open to the back and has a lovely, tailored bow at the bottom. The candle made of three clear baguettes is topped by an amber, pear-shaped flame. I have seen this same wreath done with butterscotch-colored leaves, some frosted white. 2.0" **b.** Large, pale green leaves and an open, dark red bow are the background for twelve bright red aurora borealis stones. In addition, there are two green stones and a few red enamel berries. 2.25" **c.** A simple design of two rows of stones alternating in color between siam red aurora borealis and clear red. They meet in a single ribboned knot. This is an elegant design. 2.0" **d.** This bold, brassy design by Weiss is a filigree background of mounded brass. It holds dark red and green stones in an open pattern. There is a double brass bow at the top. The same design was used on the tree in Fig 1.171. **e.** Two rows of large, faceted rhinestones, each in its own braided setting tied together at the bottom with a light green enameled bow. 2.25" $35-100 each

Fig 3.3 A lovely brass wreath by Weiss with a lacey brass bow at the top. A bell hangs free from the bow, and the clapper hangs free from the bell. Eighteen large, opaque, red cabochon holly berries embellish the large, beautifully enameled, holly leaves. 2.0" $45-115

Fig 3.4 a. This is an elegant design by Trifari. Bare branches support four pinecones and just a few stones, which are colors seen on Trifari trees—steely blue, magenta red, and green. Notice the shiny, slightly lopsided bow. 2.0" **b.** This wreath by MYLU follows the same design ideas as Fig 1.121a. Made entirely of lacey poinsettias, the design has a droopy bow riveted to the bottom flower. There are nine poinsettias, eight green stone centers. 2.62" **c.** The predominant feature of this wreath is the Mack bulldog, who sits superimposed on the bow at the top. Sold at the novelty shop of Mack Truck in Pennsylvania, not much else is known about the dates of Mack Truck Christmas pieces. This is an unsigned wreath of holly leaves and multi-colored rhinestones. 1.87" **d.** Signed *JJ*, this small wreath has green holly leaves and red enameled berries with a brushed gold bow at the top. 1.5" **e.** Large, opaque, red cabochon stone berries and green enameled leaves are riveted to a circular metal frame on this unsigned wreath. The same design appears on an unsigned tree Fig 2.27a. 1.5" $10-60 each

Fig 3.5 This wreath by Kramer is a field of chartreuse, cerise, and teal blue stones between an inner and outer ring of holly leaves. It has a gold bow at the top. 1.75" $30-60

Fig 3.6 a. Bright silver, this unsigned older, semicircular wreath supports three bells with blue stone clappers. The bells are covered in clear stones. Mixed in the green holly leaves are red cabochon berries. 1.75" **b.** This small wreath is signed, but illegibly. Welded to the top are two bells with rhinestone clappers and clear rhinestones around their rims. 1.62" **c.** Unsigned holly leaf wreath with red and green rhinestones scattered about, a gold bow at the top, and two free-hanging bells with clappers. 2.0" **d.** A lovely old piece signed *Beatrix*, this is a wreath of pine needles, poinsettias, three candles, and a bow. The candles have double rhinestones in them and their flames are tiny red stones. 1.87" **e.** An unsigned, pale gold wreath with light green leaves. There are some enameled red berries and some settings that appear to be groups of three plastic berries. The candle flame is a red navette. 2.0" **f.** A small candle wreath signed *Gerry's* has touches of red and green enameling and a bit of yellow at the flame, but no rhinestones. 1.75" $10-45 each

Fig 3.7 a. Signed *ART*, this dark green holly wreath is decorated with red cabochon berries and green rhinestones. A lovely gold-toned, ribboned bow is at the top. 2.12" **b.** Signed *Pell*, this has six holly leaf stars or perhaps poinsettias tied together with a bow at the top. The bow has a large, red square rhinestone bow knot and green baguette ribbon strips. 2.25" **c.** By MYLU, this one has just a few holly leaves strung together with red and green rhinestones and a pretty side bow. 1.75" **d.** This ART pin is enameled light green and frosted, but you can also find it in frosted dark brass. The stones buried among the foliage are similar to the colors used on ART trees—predominantly light blue, amber and orange. This has been an easy piece to find. 1.75" $10-30 each

Fig 3.8 Four contemporary wreathes, all with prong-set rhinestones. All but the second are signed *Eisenberg Ice*. **a.** Eight flower forms of red, green, and clear stones surround a clear circle. 1.75" **b.** Bauer made this candle wreath of green navettes in two sizes and red, round berries. It has an amber candle and red flame. 1.62" **c.** In this circle of red stones, navettes alternate with rounds inside a similar circle of green stones. A few red berries are scattered around the outside. 2.0" **d.** Nearly identical to the first wreath except for the red bow at the center bottom. 2.12" $30-80 each

Fig 3.9 Holiday boughs. **a.** Signed *Doddz*, this pin appeared in the Jewel Creations 1968 catalog of Christmas jewelry kits. Three white metal holly leaves with ten opaque, red cabochon holly berries. 2.25" **b.** This lovely enameled piece, signed *Sandor*, comprises just four leaves and five composition berries on a stem that twists around the base of leaves. 2.0" **c.** By Hollycraft, these three unenameled holly leaves and five siam red aurora borealis berries are tied with a large bow. 2.12" **d.** Signed *Original by Robert* but constructed much like **b**, the leaves are darker; it has composition berry beads on long stems. 2.37" **e.** A pretty pin by MYLU of two holly leaves with seven red berries on a loop of wire ribbon. 2.25" $15-50 each

Fig 3.10 a. Signed *Weiss*, a branch of dark green enameled leaves and red, opaque cabochon berries. 2.75" long **b.** A cluster of prong-set translucent red cabochons by Robert sit in four detailed, pale green leaves. 2.5" **c.** Three brushed gold leaves meet at three opaque, red cabochon berries in this pin by Trifari. 2.5" $20-60 each

Fig 3.11 a. Unsigned, this holly branch has five leaves and seventeen scattered, brilliant rhinestone berries. 2.5" **b.** A small holly branch hangs from a larger branch; red cabochon stones are glued in. Signed *JJ*. 1.75" **c.** A little pine bough signed *ART* that has four enameled green cones, a bit of frosting on the tips of the branches and just three rhinestones in typical ART colors. 2.0" **d.** This one is also signed *JJ,* and it somewhat resembles **b**. It is a short, drooping holly branch with opaque, red cabochon berries. 2.12" $15-45 each

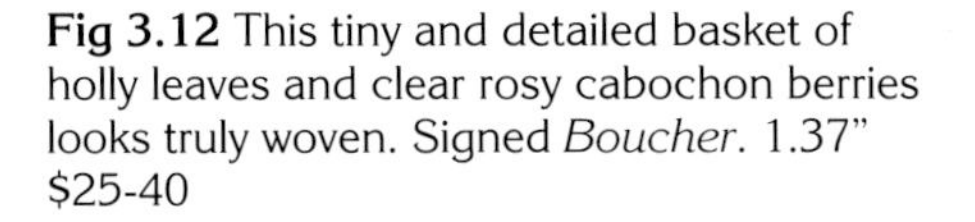

Fig 3.12 This tiny and detailed basket of holly leaves and clear rosy cabochon berries looks truly woven. Signed *Boucher*. 1.37" $25-40

Fig 3.13 a. The earrings are single-flower poinsettias on tiny green stems with a bit of foliage. They could be worn with almost any poinsettia pin. 1.37" $5-15 **b.** This is a poinsettia of very shiny red enamel with green leaves behind and seven clear rhinestones in the center. Signed *ART.* 2.0" **c.** Signed *BJ*, a three-rhinestone pot holds two poinsettias and three leaves. The center of each poinsettia is a large, amber rhinestone. 2.0" **d.** A single brass poinsettia on a long stem tied by a ribbon is signed *Beatrix*. Rhinestones adorn the flower, the leaves, and the bow. 2.62" **b-d**: $10-30 each

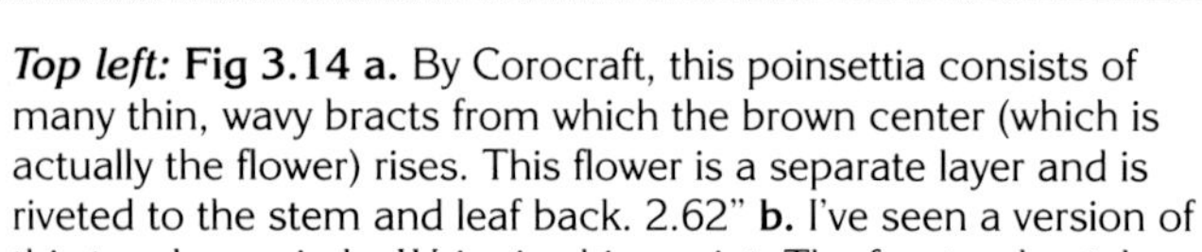

Top left: **Fig 3.14 a.** By Corocraft, this poinsettia consists of many thin, wavy bracts from which the brown center (which is actually the flower) rises. This flower is a separate layer and is riveted to the stem and leaf back. 2.62" **b.** I've seen a version of this two-layer pin by Weiss in shiny paint. The front red petals are riveted to the back leaves and stem. The center stamen in yellow and red stands high above the flower itself. It has no stones and isn't difficult to find at this time. 2.75" **c.** By Robert, this is a single-layer pin. The center is a string of yellow beads around one large orange bead. 3.0" $15-45 each

Top right: **Fig 3.15** All are unsigned except the earrings. **a.** Beautifully molded and enameled over white metal, this is a lovely poinsettia on a long stem. No rhinestones. 2.5" **b.** Very similar to the first but much larger and more detailed. 5.0" **c.** Clip-back earrings of very good quality signed *Lisner*. The petals alternate red and green. 1.37" **d.** Unsigned, but the same design idea as the earrings. 3.12" $5-25 each

Bottom right: **Fig 3.16** New in 1996, this very pretty poinsettia was purchased in San Francisco for just $5. There are four center flowers of six glittery rhinestones each to this unsigned pin. The card says "Made in Taiwan." 2.12" across $10 or less

Fig 3.17 Three baskets of poinsettias by Dorothy Bauer. All of the stones are prong-set except the flowers in the third. **a.** A handled basket with a green bow in front; the bow ribbons hang free. 2.25" **b.** Poinsettias in a low basket of open slats. 1.62" **c.** A pot of clear rhinestones, three large, twelve-petal flowers with unusual flat, translucent stones. 2.37" $85-165 each

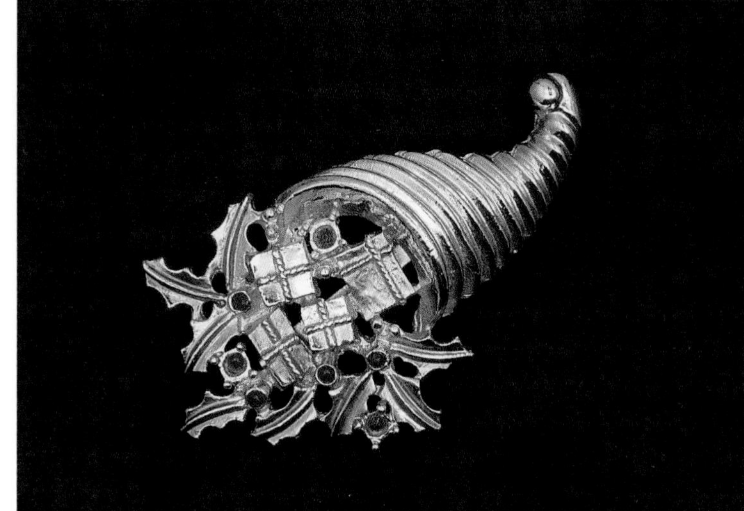

Fig 3.18 This cornucopia by BJ is filled with presents and holly. It is highlighted with seven red rhinestone berries. It is an older BJ piece. 2.37" $5-20

Chapter 4

Candles, Lanterns, and Electric Lights

Fig 4.1 Four lanterns by Hollycraft. Each of these has a glass- or possibly Lucite-enclosed candle at the top, and each has elaborate, beautiful metalwork. **a.** This is a shorter lantern, perhaps meant for carrying. With no stones, it has a large, red enamel bow and green enamel holly leaves behind it. 2.25" **b.** The base is a half-round stand just below a large, translucent carnelian-colored cabochon stone. Further up the lamp pole are a simulated pearl and an amber rhinestone. The metal is copper-colored. 3.0" **c.** Similar to **b**, but the finish is pewter, and the large, opaque stone at the bottom is gray and white, like granite. The rhinestone just above the pearl is a metallic gray. 3.0" **d.** A shorter lamp with a base, decorated with just two rhinestones on its post. 2.25" $30-85 each

Fig 4.2 a. This lantern, signed *Beatrix*, has just one red rhinestone at the knot of the red enamel bow. The back of the lantern is foiled with paper—amazing that it has survived in such good condition. The composition candle sits within the three-dimensional framework of the lantern itself. 1.62" $10-30 **b.** This ART lantern is made of gold metal, enameled black on the front of the frame. It has a red bow and green holly leaves, but no stones. 3.0" $20-40 **c.** Dorothy Bauer's lantern pin, here in black, with an unfoiled baguette for the lantern glass. The post is decorated with a round, green rhinestone wreath and a bow with ribbon chains that swing. 2.87" $45-65

Fig 4.3 Candles by ART. **a.** A large, handsome, deeply textured candle reminiscent of the ART tree in Fig 1.6b. The candle itself is done in two layers, the front hammered, the back brushed. It sits on a bed of holly leaves and pine needles. Orange stones make up the flame of the candle. 2.37" $30-45 **b.** An evergreen garland wraps this candle, which sits on a nest of boughs. Nestling in the needles are seven orange rhinestones. 2.25" $15-25 **c.** Tiny clip-back candle earrings, each with just a single stone in the flame and two that hang on the candle. They are unsigned but were bought with the matching pin. 0.75" $5-15 **d.** This set is the by now familiar ART design with rhinestone-studded stars hanging from ribbons. The pin has a two-stone flame and three stars hang down from the candle top. I have also seen this piece with a loop at the top to be worn as a pendant. 2.0" $20-35 **e.** Two candles sit above two large holly leaves, each with red, opaque cabochon berries. The candles have embossed wax drips. The tear-shaped frames around the double rhinestone flames are decorated with tiny brass knobs that add glitter to the orange rhinestones. 2.12" $15-25

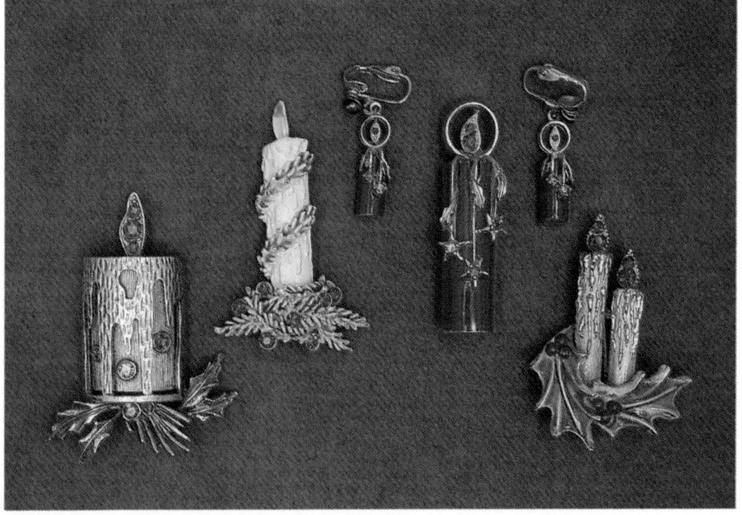

Fig 4.4 a. This is an unsigned piece in silver. Three candles, each a single amber baguette, rest on two long branches with a few leaves. Four green rhinestones sit among the foliage. 1.87" long $10-25 **b.** This piece is coated entirely in white enamel; the other colors are applied to it. Signed *Coro*, it has a single red navette stone flame. The base is large enough that it will stand alone. 1.75" $30-45 **c.** A single gold candle with large drips sits in a field of green holly leaves with red enameled berries. An orange teardrop is the flame of the piece, signed *JJ*. 1.75" $10-25 **d.** Two candles with many wax drips sit over three green leaves and three applied red berries. The flames are two amber rhinestones, each in a beaded frame. This piece is unsigned. 1.62" $10-25 **e.** In silver and signed *Beatrix*, this twisted candle sits in a bed of evergreens with the word *Noel* printed beneath it. 2.12" $10-25

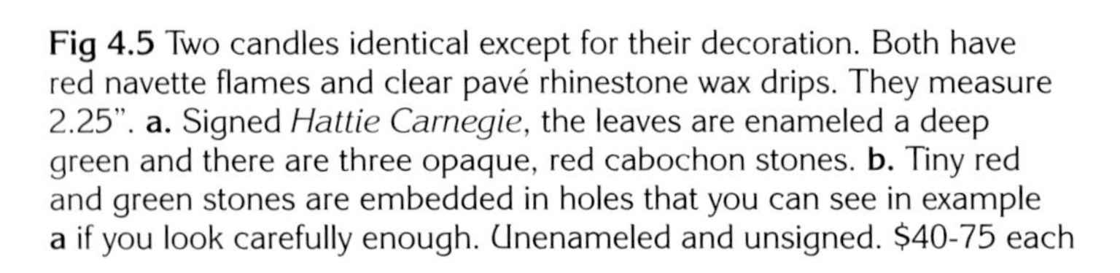

Fig 4.5 Two candles identical except for their decoration. Both have red navette flames and clear pavé rhinestone wax drips. They measure 2.25". **a.** Signed *Hattie Carnegie*, the leaves are enameled a deep green and there are three opaque, red cabochon stones. **b.** Tiny red and green stones are embedded in holes that you can see in example **a** if you look carefully enough. Unenameled and unsigned. $40-75 each

Fig 4.6 A stately candle in a traditional hand-held candlestick in this pendant by Hollycraft. Large amber navettes are centered on the candle itself, and the flame is a magenta tear. 2.25" $20-45

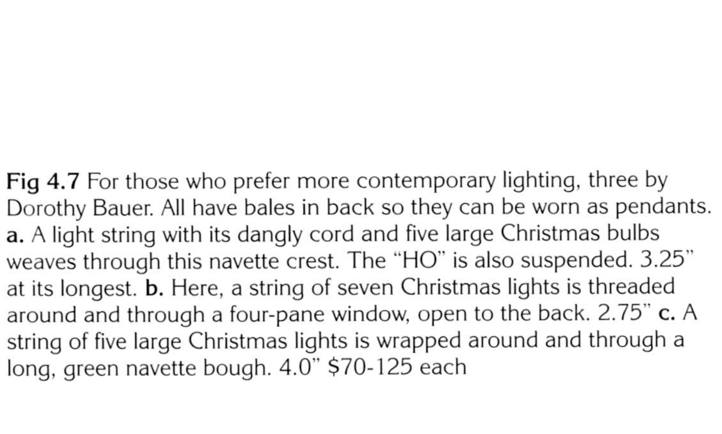

Fig 4.7 For those who prefer more contemporary lighting, three by Dorothy Bauer. All have bales in back so they can be worn as pendants. **a.** A light string with its dangly cord and five large Christmas bulbs weaves through this navette crest. The "HO" is also suspended. 3.25" at its longest. **b.** Here, a string of seven Christmas lights is threaded around and through a four-pane window, open to the back. 2.75" **c.** A string of five large Christmas lights is wrapped around and through a long, green navette bough. 4.0" $70-125 each

Chapter 5

Christmas Decorations

Fig 5.1 Three ornament-related items by Weiss. **a.** These round earrings could be worn with either of the ornament pins shown here, though they were probably designed to go with the first. Each soft-colored, round globe dangles from a large, green rhinestone applied to a clip-back earring. They are signed on the back of the globe. The ornament itself is cut by a fancy, braided ribbon and decorated with six rhinestones. 0.75" $15-40 **b.** This large, round ornament is trimmed with two fancy, braided ribbons. It hangs fixed from a short bough of holly with red enameled berries. Decorating the ornament are five large rhinestones and twelve small ones. 2.37" $40-85 **c.** Three smaller ornaments are tied to a long holly branch with dark green enamel leaves and red enamel berries. Each ornament is slightly different—two round, one pointed. Notice the large stone in the top, gold-colored ornament. It is a watermelon tourmaline that reflects the light beautifully. 2.37" at its longest $40-85

Fig 5.2 A rare and beautiful ornament pin by Hollycraft. Two bold, brass ornaments hang from evergreen boughs of a rich, deep green. At the ends of four boughs are large red or aqua cabochons. The ornaments themselves are of slightly different shapes. Both have deep horizontal grooves and rows of aqua aurora borealis rhinestones. Ringing one globe are red square stones; around the other are red round stones. 2.25" $85-165

Fig 5.3 a. This ART ornament with its turnip-like bottom is made in two layers riveted together. The back layer is a soft red color and the top layer is a gold filigree painted green around the center. It hangs by a small chain from a soft green-colored bow at the top and has no stones. 2.25" **b.** Similar to **a** in many ways, this signed *Corel* pin hangs from a chain and a bow. The ornament itself was made in two layers, the back a soft red; the front alternates vertical green stripes with open gold work. The green stripes are decorated with five tiny faux pearls; there are three clear rhinestones in the gold filigree work. 2.5" **c.** This light gold-colored ornament hangs from a simple bow. It is decorated with seventeen multi-colored rhinestones in three horizontal bands. 2.5" **d.** An unsigned ornament hangs fixed from a metal rope tying together several evergreen sprigs. A raised ribbon decoration runs across the center; six rhinestones of pale blue and amber circle its perimeter; five red rhinestones decorate the rope and sprigs. You can see the cap of the ornament at the top. 2.12" **e.** Also unsigned, this ornament is in every aspect except its color identical to Fig 5.1b. In this example the rhinestones—five large and twelve small—are larger than on the Weiss. The colors are lovely; all but the center one are aurora borealis. 2.37" $20-50 each

Fig 5.4 a. Signed *Gerry's*, it is tiny, of light, bright gold with vertical beading and raised colored knobs. At the top are three holly leaves and a bit of ribbon. 1.62" **b.** Two pastel ornaments that look very much like the two lower ornaments in Fig 5.1c weave through holly and a long pink ribbon. The softest pastel colors are used on this piece, and the fourteen rhinestones are all a pale yellow. 2.0" **c.** A brushed silver, turnip-shaped ornament signed *Doddz* and it is fixed to a bow with holly sprigs. The surface has raised scrolling and five large and four smaller stones. I have seen this unsigned in gold-finished metal. 3.0" **d.** A large, unsigned, light gold ornament decorated with rows of chartreuse rhinestones. In 1968 it was advertised in the Jewel Creations Christmas jewelry kits catalog. 2.5" **e.** This pale blue, pointed ornament is unsigned. It has the same soft-green colored holly foliage as **b.** It is cut horizontally by two raised gold bands and decorated with nine rhinestones. 2.12" $10-40 each

Fig 5.5 All of these are unsigned pieces, and none hang freely from their pin backs. **a.** The same soft red used on many of these ornaments appears here. The center, like an indent, is cut open to the back around a large amber stone. Above are a bow and holly leaves with two stones. 2.0" **b.** A similarly shaped ornament that varies at the top, which has more foliage and a rope visible to the right. The center stone of this ornament is larger. 2.0" **c.** A bright yellow ornament cut to the back in long slits and open around its central blue stone. The top of this piece looks much like **a**. 2.12" **d.** Tiny clip-back earrings that go with **e**. They have the tiniest indent with a cerise stone and six stones around it. There is also a stone in the green holly. 1.12" **e.** Similar to the earrings, though larger. You can see the ornament cap at the top, which looks much like Fig 5.3d. A large, cerise stone is set deep in the center of this lovely ornament. There are fifteen stones in all. 2.25" **f.** This ornament is divided by raised gold beading into vertical sections of green and gold. At the top are a bow and just a bit of holly. 2.25" Pins $15-35 each; earrings $5-15

Fig 5.6 Each of these Dorothy Bauer ornaments is entirely covered with stones. They can often be purchased with different color combinations. **a.** This light bulb ornament measures 1.87". **b.** A long, thin ornament with a band of vertical red navettes at the center. 2.25" **c.** Entirely round with a brass cap and a row of alternating red and green navettes at the center. 1.62" **d.** Round ornament with wire cap and alternating color stripes. 1.62" $35-60 each

Fig 5.8 A set by MYLU. **a.** These clip-back, peppermint candy earrings look good enough to eat. 1.25" $15-35 **b.** A similar peppermint candy clapper hangs freely from the candy-striped bell. The bell swings from a textured gold bow, decorated with three green holly leaves and seven red rhinestone berries. This set is guaranteed to attract comments. 3.0" $40-70

Fig 5.7 This lovely unsigned ornament was purchased newly made in 1996 for only $4. Certainly worth every penny, but you would not want to pay the price of an old ornament for it. It hangs loose from the bow top. 2.75" $10 or under

Fig 5.9 a. A bright, shiny gold bell and bow caste as a single piece and signed *Richeliu*. This is a tiny tailored piece decorated with faux pearls—a large one for the clapper and the rest distributed around the rim of the bell. 1.62" **b-c.** is a set signed *DODDZ* that was advertised as a Christmas jewelry kit by Jewel Creations in their 1968 catalog. The white metal is highlighted with gold. **b.** Earrings have three rhinestone holly berries and a holly clapper and measure 1.12". **c.** A metal ribbon is threaded through the loop tops to hold three bells. Holly leaves and five berries above and three red rhinestone clappers. 2.0" at the longest dimension. **d.** A lovely bell by Corel that swings from a metal bow. The knot is covered with small red rhinestones. It has embossed green holly and three red rhinestone berries. A faceted, clear, iridescent, tear-shaped stone hangs free between the front and back of the metal bell, so it actually tinkles when it moves. 2.25" Pins $15-30; earrings $5-15 each

Fig 5.10 These three bells all have iridescent siam red stones. **a.** An unsigned silver metal bell with a loop at the top, covered with rhinestones just slightly open to the back. The rhinestone-set clapper hangs free. Similarly shaped earrings with screw back (not shown) match this pin. 2.12" **b.** This Hollycraft piece combines holly leaves, bow, and bell decorated with just two large stones. 2.5" **c.** This lovely piece by Beatrix is quite heavy. The large stones at the bottom are red aurora borealis, and there is another row of rhinestones midway up the bell. The bottom half is cut to the back in geometric designs. 2.37" $20-50 each

Fig 5.11 Here is the Hollycraft bell from Fig 5.10b as a pendant. 2.5" $20-40

Fig 5.12 a. This bell with its attractive scroll-cut center section hangs from the bow above. Its clapper is faceted plastic. It is signed *Gerry's* and measures 2.37". **b.** This tiny rhinestone-covered bell dangles from five holly leaves. The rhinestone clapper is fixed. Signed *Doddz*, it was advertised in the 1968 Jewel Creations catalog as a Christmas jewelry kit. 1.5" **c.** A white bell by ART hangs free from its bundle of greens. Four stars hang in ribbons from the top of the bell. At the center of each is a rhinestone. Notice the similarity of the design to the tree Fig 1.7c and to the candle Fig 4.3b. 2.0" **d.** A red bell with a faux pearl clapper hangs from a ribbon and green holly leaves. Signed *ART*. 2.0" **e.** An unusual design by BJ, half of this bell is open lattice, the other half is textured gold. The clapper is fixed and the bell is suspended from two short, wide lengths of ribbon. 3.25" **f.** This MYLU bell hangs loose from the sculptured bow; the clapper also hangs free. It has a fish-scale design, and each scale holds a clear, iridescent rhinestone—forty in all. 2.12" $15-35 each

Fig 5.13 This bell is similar to Fig 5.12f and is also by MYLU. On both, the bow is the same. Here, the bell is made entirely of holly leaves cut open to the back. There are ten rhinestone berries in the holly. 2.12" $30-60

Fig 5.14 a. Holly leaves with long red stems and red berries support a chain of six bells. The berries and the chain total thirteen red rhinestones. 3.0" **b.** Two bells with red faceted bead clappers hang from a bow in this unsigned piece. The bells have clear stones around their rims. 2.12" **c.** This unusual bell by BJ has googly eyes that jiggle. It is suspended from holly leaves. There are ten clear rhinestones on the clapper which hangs free. 1.62" **d.** A double-outline bell with the clapper support down the center. The clapper is fixed. 1.75" $15-40 each

Fig 5.15 These two rhinestone-covered pieces are both signed *Dorothy Bauer*. **a.** Two lovely white bells hang free from holly leaves and three berries. The bells themselves are trimmed in red and the clappers are fixed. It could also be worn as a pendant. 2.5" $65-95 **b.** Mostly dark green and against silver metal, this flat bell with red stripes has a large red clapper. 2.12" $25-40

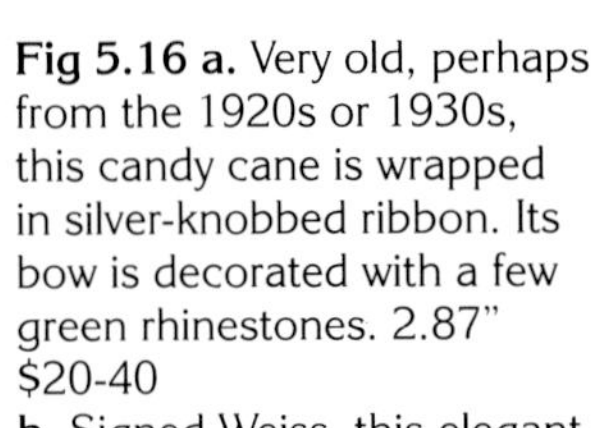

Fig 5.16 a. Very old, perhaps from the 1920s or 1930s, this candy cane is wrapped in silver-knobbed ribbon. Its bow is decorated with a few green rhinestones. 2.87" $20-40
b. Signed Weiss, this elegant candy cane alternates sections of deep red rhinestones with pairs of clear baguettes. It is wrapped in the center with a double-looped bow. 2.62" $40-70

Fig 5.17 a. This tiny, enameled cane is signed *Hollycraft* on the back. I have also seen it without its enamel. It has five holly berries and two green aurora borealis stones in the holly cluster at its center. 1.75" **b.** Signed *Tancer II*, this candy cane has gold and red stripes. The bow is decorated with a lovely domed, star-shaped, aurora borealis rhinestone. 2.5" **c.** A rhinestone-covered candy cane by Dorothy Bauer. The ribbons on the bow hang loose. 3.25" **d.** Rows of rhinestones form the stripes of these two candy canes, wrapped in a bow and holiday greens. Unsigned. 2.0" $15-50 each

Fig 5.18 This lovely old, high-topped, Victorian lady's boot is signed *Original by Robert*. The boot itself is enameled red with black trim. Green holly and red berries decorate the top. It is just 1.62". $85-145

Fig 5.19 a. Small cuffed boot in silver metal contains three packages and holly. No rhinestones, signed *ART*. 1.5" $5-20 **b.** Beautiful brushed stocking with a red enamel cuffed top. We can see a candy cane, holly, and some lovely rhinestones at the top. Signed *Weiss*. 2.75" $45-65 **c.** An unsigned pin of two layers, the front layer has a few red rhinestones and nine large scalloped watermelon tourmaline beads, each topped with a clear prong-set rhinestone. These are threaded through the top layer of the stocking. 2.5" $5-20

Fig 5.20 This imaginative, unsigned piece is composed entirely of toys and Christmas symbols, cut open to the back between them. You can see a horse, a locomotive, Christmas stocking, baby buggy, and pinecones, among other items. This resembles a tree signed *Raffine*, not pictured. 2.37" $20-40

Fig 5.21 a. Although signed *Weiss* on the back, I suspect this is a new piece. Done in silver metal, it is almost entirely flat. The packages form a back layer and the bow is layered above it, with ribbon ends that hang. It does not look like the kind of work for which the old Weiss was famous. 2.5" **b.** Unsigned and completely flat, this amusing stocking with its toe and heel patches is decorated with just a little holly at its upper edge. This is a new piece. 2.87" $20-45 each

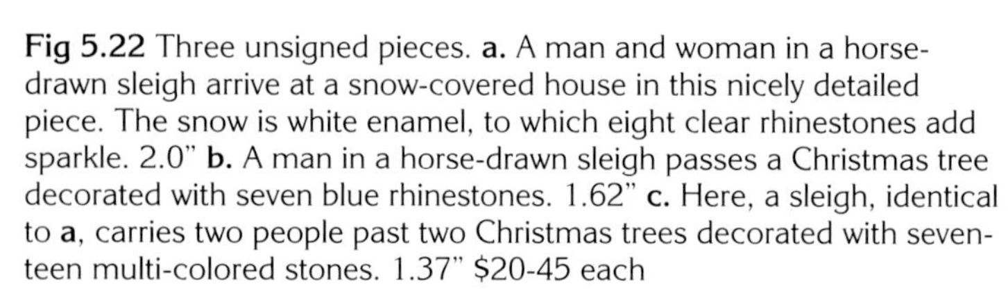

Fig 5.22 Three unsigned pieces. **a.** A man and woman in a horse-drawn sleigh arrive at a snow-covered house in this nicely detailed piece. The snow is white enamel, to which eight clear rhinestones add sparkle. 2.0" **b.** A man in a horse-drawn sleigh passes a Christmas tree decorated with seven blue rhinestones. 1.62" **c.** Here, a sleigh, identical to **a**, carries two people past two Christmas trees decorated with seventeen multi-colored stones. 1.37" $20-45 each

Fig 5.23 a. A detailed, dark brass church with a movable bell in its tower and baguette glass windows stands in the snow. Nine clear rhinestones made the snow glitter, and there is a red rhinestone where the rose window might be. This unsigned piece looks like it was made by the same manufacturer as Fig 5.22a. 2.0" $30-60 **b.** A door with a tiny Christmas tree finial above it. A wreath hangs from a chain in the upper half of the door. Unsigned. 2.5" $15-25 **c.** A white enamel fireplace, signed *Doddz*, with andirons, two stockings, and holly. This piece was offered as a jewelry kit in the 1968 Jewel Creations catalog. It can also be found in a bright gold finish. 1.62" $15-40

Fig 5.24 This pin by JJ has been reissued several times in the 1990s. It is a 2.25" hinged door with a green wreath and red bow that opens to reveal...

Fig 5.25 ...two children coming down Christmas morning, their stockings filled, their dog sitting by the tree, and a candle on the mantelpiece. The section around the stair railing and the children is open to the back. $30-55

Chapter 6

Animals

Fig 6.2 This Hollycraft deer is identical to Fig 6.1a except for the color of the stones in the antlers. Here he appears in a frilly, tear-shaped loop intended to be worn as a pendant. 2.25" $20-45

Fig 6.1 In this picture, **a** and **c** are versions of the tiny Hollycraft deer. The same deer is also featured in Fig 6.2. **a.** Wears a harness of aurora borealis rhinestones and has a tiny, red stone eye and brown stones in his antlers. 1.75" **b.** This large deer is a lovely piece by MY-LU—obviously Rudolph with a large cabochon nose. He has painted holly and berries around his neck, a green navette eye, and long eyelashes. Six iridescent stones dangle from his antlers. 3.0" **c.** This deer differs from **a** in coloration, colored stones, and in the fact that he has two stones hanging from his antlers. Some of his brown enamel has worn off. 1.75" $25-50 each

Fig 6.4 a. By MYLU, he wears a holly wreath around his neck, green holly leaves, and red rhinestone berries. He has a tomato-red cabochon nose and a green navette eye. He looks more like Bambi than a full-grown deer. 2.25" **b.** Signed *Tancer II*, this is a deer head in very light, bright gold with curly antlers and a wreath of poinsettias—styled much like a MYLU tree. At the centers of the poinsettias are green stones—nine of them. In addition, he has a green navette eye. 2.75" **c.** This is an older Gerry's piece, a reindeer head above a small green enameled wreath with painted red berries. He (she?) also looks like an immature deer. The only stone is a round, green eye. 2.75" $15-35 each

Fig 6.3 a. Signed *Kramer*, this is a beautifully crafted reindeer head with a red cabochon nose and eyes; the irises are cut to the back. The enameled head and antlers are in lovely condition and there is a V-shaped patch of rhinestones on its forehead—twenty-two stones in all. 2.5" $45-75 **b.** Unsigned, at one time this handsome reindeer had a red nose, but no stones ever. He wears green holly in his antlers and his coat is brushed with white. 2.25" **c.** A stylized version of Rudolph has a bell hanging free from his ear, long eyelashes, and a tomato-like cabochon for a nose. He wears a green sweater. Signed *Corel*. 3.37" **d.** Unsigned bright, light gold frontal view of a reindeer. He has green eyes and holly leaves and tiny red rhinestone berries—twelve stones in all. 2.25" **b-d**: $15-55 each

Fig 6.5 Two signed deer heads above small holly wreathes, both have red noses and antlers. **a.** Signed *ART*, has long, curved eyelashes and a red navette eye. There are four rhinestones in the holly. 2.0" **b.** Signed *Gerry's*, this one has a circular, green stone eye and enamel berries. 2.0" $15-25 each

Fig 6.6 Five reindeer. **a.** A prancing white-enameled deer has red antlers and nose. There are no stones; he is signed *ART*. 2.12" $40-60 **b.** This leaping reindeer by Hedy has white antlers and hooves and a rhinestone collar. There are seven stones including the one in his eye. 2.75" **c.** Three tiny reindeer with red antlers and collars and red rhinestone eyes prance in step. 1.75" long **d.** This unsigned green-eyed deer sits beside a tree on a snowy ledge decorated with clear rhinestones. His coat is brushed with green and is decorated with tiny colored rhinestones. 2.25" **e.** The very same deer, in a slightly different finish, signed *JJ*, sits without the tree or base. He does have the green rhinestone eyes. 1.75" **b-e**: $15-35 each

Fig 6.7 a. This deer is enameled in white and trimmed with green holly and berries. He is unsigned and has no rhinestones, but he is obviously Rudolph. 3.5" in his longest dimension **b.** This unsigned comic reindeer struggles with his Christmas shopping duties. His large package is decorated with eight red cabochons. 2.5" **c.** A tiny, Gerry's leaping deer with green holly leaves and red berries in his mouth. He has textured tail, ear, and hooves and a green rhinestone eye. Signed *Gerrys*. 2.5" **d.** Signed *MYLU*, he is a flat, stylized deer and has at his neck two holly leaves and a fixed bell. The rim of this bell is decorated with stones. Here he has a clear baguette eye, but I have also seen him with a red navette eye. 2.37" **e.** This Boucher deer leaps over a decorated Christmas tree, a package, and a hat box. The deer has a red stone nose and clear rhinestones on his body. The tree is also decorated. 2.5" $10-45 each

Fig 6.8 Four pieces by JJ decorated with tiny rhinestones. **a.** A tiny mouse in a Santa suit carries a tinier Christmas tree over his shoulder. He has a green eye and clear rhinestone trim. The tree is brushed with green and has little colored rhinestones nearly flush with the surface. There are twenty-six stones in all. 1.62" **b.** Framed in this holly wreath with red rhinestone berries are the head and paws of a kitten. His feet support the wreath and we see his tail to the side. The berries are red rhinestones; there are clear rhinestones around his hat and at the bow knot; his eyes are green. 1.75" **c.** Here, a mouse's head and feet are framed by the wreath. His long tail curls up along the side. 1.62" **d.** A cocky kitten with a tree in the crook of his arm faces front, his hat pulled down over one eye. 1.5" $50-85 each

Fig 6.10 a. Signed *LG* in a palette-shaped cartouche, Santa Mouse, decorated with just two green rhinestone eyes, holds a Christmas tree in his extended left hand. 1.62" **b.** This mouse lies on a toboggan, his pink scarf flying in the breeze. He has a single cerise rhinestone in his eye. 1.75" **c.** A lady mouse in a Christmas tree skirt coyly holds her long tail in her right hand. Her mouth and eyes are cut open to the back. She has no rhinestones and is unsigned. 1.75" **d.** Just the head of this mouse shows out of a Christmas stocking, signed *JJ*. He has red rhinestone eyes and a bit of holly on either side. 1.87" $30-55 each

Fig 6.9 A rotund mouse hoists a potted Christmas tree in his left hand. He has long whiskers, an opaque red nose, and black rhinestone eyes. Eleven rhinestones decorate his tree. He's a charmer. 2.25" $30-50

Fig 6.11 a. Perhaps more doll than animal, this looks a bit like Raggedy Ann on a bad hair day. Signed *Corel*, her dress is red and in her hair is green holly decorated with three red stones. 2.0" **b.** Like Ms. Mouse in Fig 6.10c, this charmer primps in her Christmas tree dress. She has holly and three red berries in her hair, no paint, and is signed *Corel*. 2.12" **c.** This unsigned mouse in pixie shoes and a Santa cap carries a sprig of holly in the crook of his left arm. He has green rhinestone eyes. 1.87" $20-50 each

Fig 6.12. Five holiday mice, each signed *BJ*. All are in a pale gold finish except the largest, which is silver. **a.** Arms and legs outstretched, this little boy mouse wears a green sweater and red pants. 1.37" **b.** This pin is a trembler—the head bears the pin back and the body is attached to it by a spring. He will jiggle when his wearer moves. His belt and the rim of his cap bear the only stones to be found on these five mice. 2.0" **c.** This little girl mouse has flirty eyes and a short-sleeved sweater, which she fills with curves unusual in a rodent. 1.37" **d.** The same boy mouse on a toboggan is so confidant that he holds on with just one hand. 1.75" at its longest dimension. **e.** Here, our mouse seems completely out of control on his skis. 1.5" $15-30 each

Fig 6.13 a. A red-enameled stocking by ART is elaborately decorated with tassels and raised designs. Santa has filled it with a candy cane, holly, faux pearls, and a small kitten with blue eyes. 2.37" **b.** I'm not sure what to call this unusual animal in a Santa hat. He holds a big candy cane with holly and three blue berries. He is unsigned and has aqua cabochon eyes. 2.0" **c.** A duck in profile carries an enormous candy cane with lovely detailing. He has aqua cabochon eyes. His cap has faux pearls around its rim and a pompon covered with tiny faux pearls. This is a particularly well-detailed piece. 1.37" **d.** A green-eyed kitten pulls a rhinestone-covered tree on a red sled. The tree is entirely covered with green flat-backed stones. The piece is unsigned and is 2.25" in its longest dimension. $15-35 each

Fig 6.14 Four little pins for dog lovers. **a.** This dachshund is decked out for Christmas. He wears holly leaves and three poinsettias on his head. He has a green eye and there are four green poinsettia centers, as well. Signed *P.I.M.*, at his longest he measures 2.0". $40-65 **b.** This poodle wears a red Santa hat and sits with a candy cane in his mouth. There are no stones on this pin signed *Corel*. 1.75" **c.** A dog (a terrier?) sits in a Santa hat; on the tassel are green holly leaves. He has a green bow around his neck but no stones. Signed *Corel*. 1.75" **d.** In a similar pose with a green bow and a Santa hat sits this tiny Gerry's dog with green rhinestone eyes. 1.5" **b-d**: $15-45 each

Fig 6.15 Three dogs in boots. **a.** Above the rim of this boot we see the head, one foreleg, and a paw of a puppy of uncertain parentage. The boot hangs from a green rhinestone bow, and its top is decorated with clear iridescent stones. This boot is painted a shiny red and is signed *Weiss*. I have seen the identical piece without the iridescent stones, unsigned. 1.87" **b.** A small poodle in a decorated boot is signed *Gerry's*. 1.75" **c.** This is the famous MYLU movable poodle in a boot. A rivet in back allows the poodle to rock from side to side. It is a very nicely molded poodle with red eyes and three rhinestones in its collar. On a similar unsigned piece, the dog doesn't move and there is less detail and no rhinestones. 1.87" $15-45 each

Fig 6.16 In this outstanding piece by MYLU, a leopard with green rhinestone eyes and dark rhinestone spots proudly sits for his portrait. He wears a crown decorated with red rhinestones and a bow tie of green holly leaves knotted with a clear rhinestone. 2.87" from crown to tip of his tail. $55-135

Fig 6.17 Four pins from 'toon town. **a.** Pluto lives it up on the ice pond in this older pin. He is wearing his best Christmas scarf. Signed *Walt Disney Productions*. 1.75" $50-95 **b.** Tweety bird tries to hoist an enormous Christmas ornament made even heavier by twenty-two rhinestones. Signed *Warner Bros*. 2.0" **c.** Bugs Bunny gingerly transports a tray of Christmas ornaments— probably to his tree. Careful, Bugs! Signed *Warner Bros*. 2.25" **d.** Donald, Mickey, and Goofy proudly bring their Christmas tree home. Notice who got conned into carrying the heavy end. Signed *Disney/Napier*. 2.5" long. **b-d**: $20-55 each

Fig 6.18 A lovely MYLU dove of peace carries a holly bough that has five red rhinestone berries. The metal wings have been lightly hammered, then brushed to give texture to this truly elegant piece. 2.25" $30-65

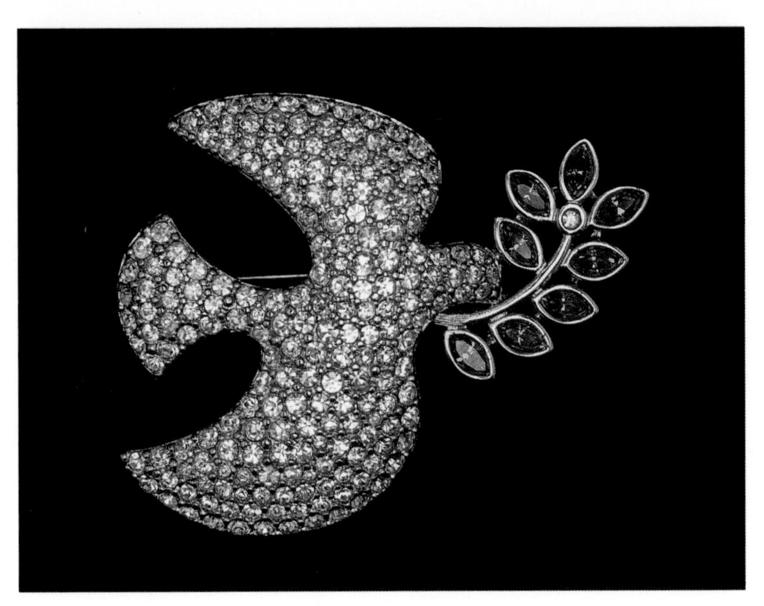

Fig 6.19 Swarovski's elegant peace dove carries an olive branch. The bird is entirely covered with clear pavé stones. The leaves on the branch are amber navettes. The back of the pin is filled with a red-brown enamel. Like other Swarovski pins, it is signed with the figure of a swan. This was made in 1995 in an edition limited to 655 pieces and sold new for $135. 2.25" $175+

Fig 6.20 Four trees by Cadaro. Notice that on three of the four trees, the birds are identical. **a.** This is a round topiary tree, partly enameled green, in an aqua pot with a red bow around its trunk. There are two enameled pears and five red cabochon stones. The blue partridge is applied to the tree. 2.87" $45-110 **b.** Here is an elegantly enameled broadleaf with two yellow pears and an applied bird in pavé clear rhinestones with a red rhinestone eye—three tiny rhinestones in all. 2.5" $85-145 **c.** A tall triangular tree with a few leaves and sixteen gold-tone pears. It, too, has a blue partridge. 2.75" $45-110 **d.** Seven yellow pears hang from this much-pruned pear tree, which has only a few green leaves left. The bird perches on one of the bare branches. 2.37" $45-110

Fig 6.23 Here are two unsigned partridges in pear trees. **a.** Looks nearly identical to the Cadaro in Fig 6.20d, but with fewer rhinestones on the body of the bird. It has a red stone eye. 2.5" $30-85
b. A cruder example of the same tree. Although there are clear stones on the bird and one red one, the red isn't in the correct position to be the bird's eye. 2.37" $15-35

Top left: **Fig 6.21 a.** A gold partridge and two gold pears are applied on top of this two-layer, deciduous tree by Robert. We've seen this tree before, decorated with hanging beads, in Fig 1.134a. 2.5" $60-120 **b.** This tree is pictured on its original card, which says *England* and *Corel*. The partridge, signed *Corel*, sits on a short branch from which hangs a faceted, clear, pear-shaped aurora borealis bead. 2.25" **c.** Signed *MYLU*, variations of this pin have the bird sitting on a branch with different types of leaves, sometimes serrated, sometimes smooth. This bird has a red eye. A lovely opalescent faceted stone that is pear-shaped but flat on the bottom dangles from the branch. 2.25" **b-c**: $20-40 each

Bottom left: **Fig 6.22**. **a.** The enameled bird, here cream-colored, is sometimes tan. He floats over an odd tree that has both pears and red berries—probably grafted. The foliage is very pale green, and the pin is signed *ART*. 2.0" **b.** In this pin by Accessocraft, the bird, a bit of red paint on his wings, sits on a tree with light green leaves and six yellow pears. It has no stones and measures 2.75". **c.** A brown enameled bird sits on a light gold branch with green leaves. Signed *BJ*, he has a red stone eye. The length of this pin is 2.87". $15-40 each

Fig 6.24 a. Partridge/pear trees wouldn't be complete without at least one pair of turtle doves. So here are two turtle doves on a branch over four dangly, decorated ornaments. No rhinestones on this pin signed *Corel*. 2.0" $45-85. **b.** Signed *Beatrix*, it is a flat tree with an enameled poinsettia top, a single yellow pear, and partridge. Each section is outlined to define the paint areas. 2.5" $20-40

Fig 6.25 This is a group of pins on a Western theme by Don Lin. They are modestly priced and are available in some Texas department stores and from other dealers. The armadillo in the Santa hat has a particular charm. Just the present for friends who like to gather 'round the Yule-tide cactus and sing cowboy carols. $10-20 each

Chapter 7

Santas and Sleighs

Fig 7.1 Here are two Santas that might also be described as Christmas trees. The molding is nearly identical, but they are decorated quite differently. Both are cut through to the back under the eyes and through the mouth. Both have wide, decorated belts, and an ornament top. 2.5" each **a.** Signed *Hollycraft*, the back of this piece is brightly colored brass; the front is deeply textured. All of the rhinestones are red, including the eyes; there are also faux pearls. **b.** Signed *Alice Caviness*. This is decorated with small, round, red and green rhinestones. $95-225 each

Fig 7.2 Two Santa Claus pendants by Hollycraft. **a.** In profile, Santa carries a large bundle decorated with colored rhinestones on a stick over his back. He has a row of baguettes around the bottom of his short coat, and he is surrounded by a filigreed frame. This was also made as a pin without the frame and can be found with enamel paint. 2.25" **b.** Santa rides a reindeer—no hands—in this pendant. He is enameled red with black boots and white trim. His reindeer has a red rhinestone eye. Also available unenameled. 2.25" $35-100 each

Fig 7.3 a. Signed *Weiss*, this Santa stands facing forward, decorated with tiny rhinestones around his cap, wrists, and on his boots. He has a red nose, mouth, and enameled red tassel. His eyes are green rhinestones. 2.12" $60-110 **b.** This unsigned piece was certainly made by the same manufacturer as **a**—he has the same rhinestone trim, green eyes, and red tassel on his hat. Here he waves his left hand. 2.12" **c.** A jolly, fat Santa has a wassail bowl. This piece is signed *Corel* and is unadorned by rhinestones. 1.75" **d.** Signed *Raffine*, Santa is perhaps a chef offering a holiday menu. 2.25" b-d: $25-50 each

Fig 7.4 Each of these poses the question, is the pin a Santa or a Christmas tree? In each case, Santa is triangular and has a decoration at his top. **a.** Signed *Corel*, Santa has a white beard and one green eye; he is winking. 2.0" **b.** Santa is dressed as a Christmas tree—no other explanation for this kind of outlandishness. 2.0" **c.** Signed *MYLU*, this is quite a bit like **a**. This time there is a star at the top; Santa has both eyes straight ahead. 2.5" $20-45 each

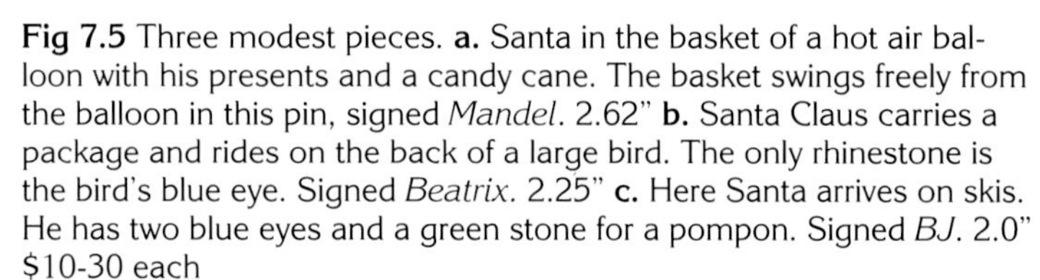

Fig 7.5 Three modest pieces. **a.** Santa in the basket of a hot air balloon with his presents and a candy cane. The basket swings freely from the balloon in this pin, signed *Mandel*. 2.62" **b.** Santa Claus carries a package and rides on the back of a large bird. The only rhinestone is the bird's blue eye. Signed *Beatrix*. 2.25" **c.** Here Santa arrives on skis. He has two blue eyes and a green stone for a pompon. Signed *BJ*. 2.0" $10-30 each

Fig 7.6 a. Santa with a rather puzzled look on his face sits in the sleigh. Signed *Doddz*, this piece was offered in the 1968 catalog from Jewel Creations as a Christmas jewelry kit. 1.62" **b.** On this unsigned stick-pin, a blue-eyed Santa carries a small lantern in the crook of his right arm. Other than the lantern, he looks a bit like a smaller version of Fig 7.3b. 1.62" **c.** A roly-poly Santa with two green eyes, signed *ART*. It is enameled on the front. Face and red rim are riveted to the back layer. 1.62" **d.** Santa in the frame of a tree, which is decorated with holly and berries at the top. Santa's white rhinestone eyes seem to twinkle. This pin is signed *Beatrix*. 2.5" **e.** Santa's torso is seen rising from (or descending into) a chimney top in this piece with a pewter-like finish. It is signed *IS 1974*. 2.75" **f.** An ART profile of Santa carrying a large pack of packages on his back. The packages are painted; there are three rhinestones tucked in among them. 1.75" $10-45 each

Fig 7.7 All the stones on these two heads are prong-set. In each case, the beard hangs loosely. **a.** This lovely old piece is signed *Hobé 1965* on a cartouche. The eyes, nose, and moustache are layered above the face proper. 2.5" $90-175 **b.** This current design by Bauer is entirely flat. Santa has a pointed hat and a beard composed of chains of rhinestones. 2.87" $55-85

Fig 7.8 Kirk's Folly made only 300 copies of this piece, but it was still available as of this writing. It is composed of prong-set rhinestones. The beard curls slightly because the rhinestone chains of which it is made are soldered or glued together at the bottom, loose higher up. Here, Santa has an open mouth, a very large red nose and a lot of charm. 3.5" $95-150

Fig 7.9 A Santa and fantasy Night Before Christmas piece by Lunch at the Ritz has everything—the sun, stars, Santa, a sleigh, a Christmas tree, packages, stockings, rocking horse, and lots of glitz and style. The enamel is epoxy-coated to make it more durable. 4.5" $300-450

Fig 7.10 What happens to Santa's hat when he's having those cookies? DeNicola has thought of everything. Here's a hat rack with many stylish hats, and Santa has deposited a rhinestone-covered one for his short stay. 2.25" $95-200

Fig 7.11 Six of the many sleighs Santa has to choose from. **a.** Rhinestone-bedecked, three bells hang from the runners, possibly slowing its progress. Red packages sit in the back of this unsigned sleigh. 2.0" long **b.** A simple, small sleigh with scrollwork attached to the runners, this pin is decorated with clear rhinestones and has a red carriage lamp. Unsigned. 1.5" **c.** Probably the most commonly found sleigh, this pretty one is red with three packages, each with its own rhinestone-trimmed bow. Signed *Tancer II*, it is sometimes decorated differently, sometimes unpainted. A slightly different version, but with the same molding, can be found signed *MYLU*. 1.5" **d.** A galloping horse pulls a sleigh that carries a Christmas tree. The horse's eye is red and there are six more stones, four of them decorating the tree. 2.75" **e.** A high-backed red sleigh, its edges trimmed with red rhinestones, carries a frosted, decorated Christmas tree. When I'm describing a sleigh over the telephone or by e-mail, I like to say whether it is going east or west. This one is going east. 1.62" **f.** Signed *MYLU*, this sleigh carries a large, bow-wrapped, striped candy cane. It is going east. 1.75" long $25-60 each

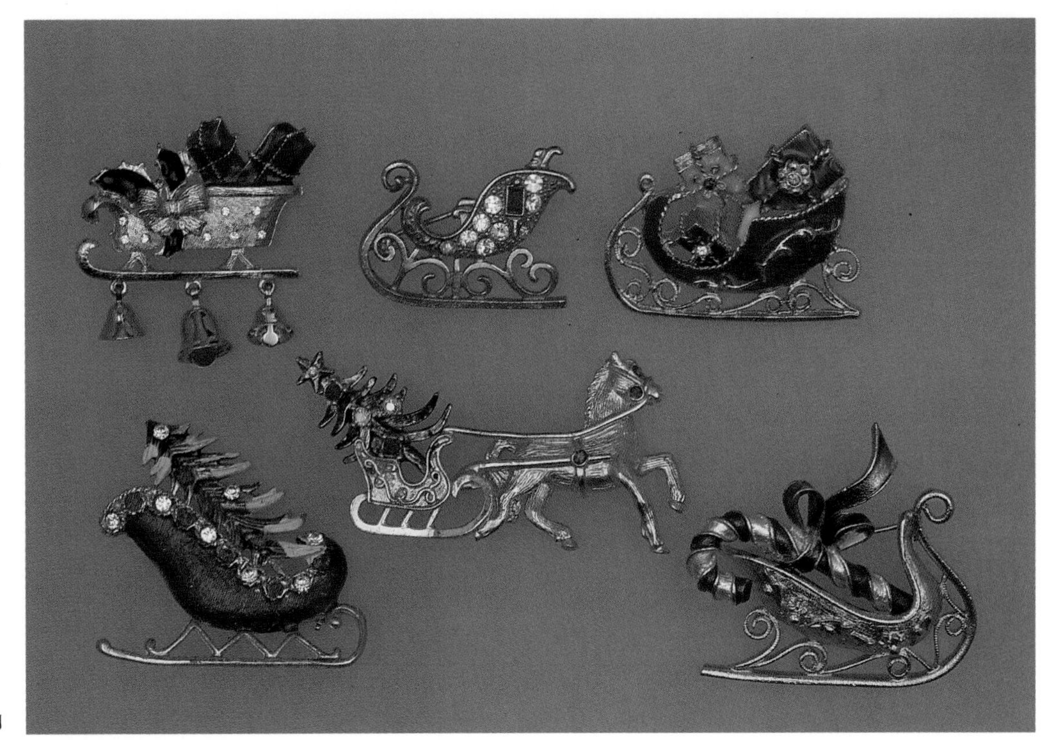

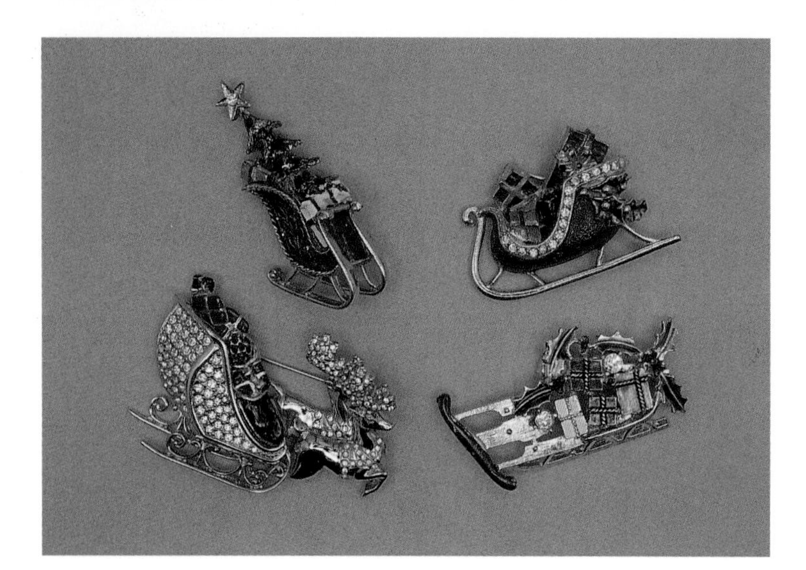

Fig 7.12 a. Here is a three-dimensional sleigh that seems to be slipping right off the wearer's coat. It carries packages and a tree and is very tall for its length. Unsigned. 2.12" $15-35
b. Signed *St Labre*, this red sleigh has three packages and holly leaves that trail from its back. Its rim is decorated with clear rhinestones. 1.75" $35-55 **c.** I am uncertain how old this sleigh by Swarovski is. The sleigh, the reindeer's antlers, and their harnesses are clear pavé rhinestones. The hat is red rhinestones and the packages are red and green. This is a lovely pin that is not currently available, at least in the United States. 2.25" long $140-180 **d.** This probably doesn't qualify as a Santa sleigh, but it might do in a pinch. The sled, signed *Weiss,* is covered with colorful packages, holly, and two clear rhinestones. It measures 2.0" long. $30-45

Fig 7.13 Two pieces by Bauer. **a.** These two pins are attached chatelaine-style. Rudolph and the sleigh have separate pin backs and are attached by a dangly chain. 4.25" at its greatest. $70-95 **b.** Maybe Santa wouldn't have used this wagon to bring the Christmas tree, but it is a nice idea. The wheels are attached on tiny axles so they spin freely. 2.25" long $55-110

Chapter 8

Snowmen, Angels, and Other Figures

Fig 8.1 Here are seven imaginative snowmen, all signed. **a.** Made of two simple round white snowballs and a derby hat, this guy is decorated with a baguette bow tie and a candy cane. He has four black rhinestones for buttons and eyes. *Weiss.* 2.0" $25-60 **b.** This Weiss snowman runs carrying a pearl snowball. Rhinestones decorate his red scarf and stovepipe hat. 1.75" $85-125 **c.** This opalescent, enameled snowman with a carrot nose carries a broom. He was created by Carolee. 1.5" $45-80 **d.** A snowman signed *H (in a Heart)*, but outside the heart is written *edy*, which has led me to believe that H (in a Heart) and Hedy are probably one in the same. The stylized H in the hearts are identical. This snowman sports holly in his hat, carries a Christmas tree, and has six rhinestones. 2.0" $40-60 **e.** Signed *Hollycraft* and carrying a small Christmas tree fixed in his left arm; dangling from his right arm is a little plastic Christmas package. His eyes and buttons are rhinestones. 1.75" $45-85 **f.** This wonderful MYLU snowman, in a gold bow tie and holly-decorated gold top hat, flies along on very long skis. He seems to know just what to do with his snow arms to stay balanced in mid-air. Five rhinestones in his holly, his bow knot, and his eyes. 2.0" $65-125 **g.** A brassy gold piece is signed *Raffine.* The snowman with a large cane (of candy) stands on a snow mound beside a building and under an old-fashioned street lamp. No rhinestones. 2.12" $15-35

Fig 8.2 Three items. **a.** Signed *Beatrix*, the metal is all white. It is hard to know whether this is a snowman or a winter scarecrow. The figure is covered in white-outlined holly leaves with red composition berries. I've seen another example in gold-tone metal with just a few red rhinestones and a collar and hat of green rhinestones. 1.87" **b.** This unsigned snowman carries a small, detailed Christmas tree and sports a scarf. Holly berries and leaves adorn his hat. He has rhinestone buttons, nose, and eyes. 1.87" **c.** A jaunty snowman, signed *Doddz*, has special snowman feet. He carries a broom upright. His three buttons are black rhinestones and he has red rhinestone eyes. He is all-white metal, front and back, with gold highlights. 1.62" $15-55 each

Fig 8.3 Two snowperson pins by Carolee. **a.** He has a rounded body covered with pave rhinestones, gold buttons, and an enameled black and gold trimmed scarf and hat. This 1994 piece was limited to 500 examples and sold new for $115. 2.12" $125-165 **b.** A happy couple, their heads and bottom rounds are faux pearls. Their middle section, where they huddle together (certainly not for warmth), is metal. She looks as if she has had her hair done for the occasion, and he wears his best scarf, which is touched with red enamel. 1.5" $45-75

Opposite page, right: **Fig 8.4** A jaunty, giant, limited edition snowman by Kirk's Folly. Although only 500 of this piece were made, he was still available as of this writing. You can see the ice crystals that dangle from his stick arms, the red rhinestone band around his hat, and the metal flower. What may be less clear is his large pointed nose that extends nearly half an inch in front of him. He was definitely the work of a creative mind. 5.5" $175-250

Fig 8.5 a. This snowman by Lunch at the Ritz has three separate sections chain-linked together. His white enamel has been glittered as well as encircled by clear rhinestones. He carries a broom in one stick hand, ice crystals and a snowflake in the other. Notice the orange rhinestone at the end of his long, bright orange carrot nose. Currently available and very stylish. 3.87" $185-220
b. By Kirk's Folly, this fellow smokes a pipe, a dangerous habit for any snowman. A tiny fairy adjusts his stovepipe hat. He is covered with clear aurora borealis stones, and snow flakes hang from his body. 4.37" $28-45

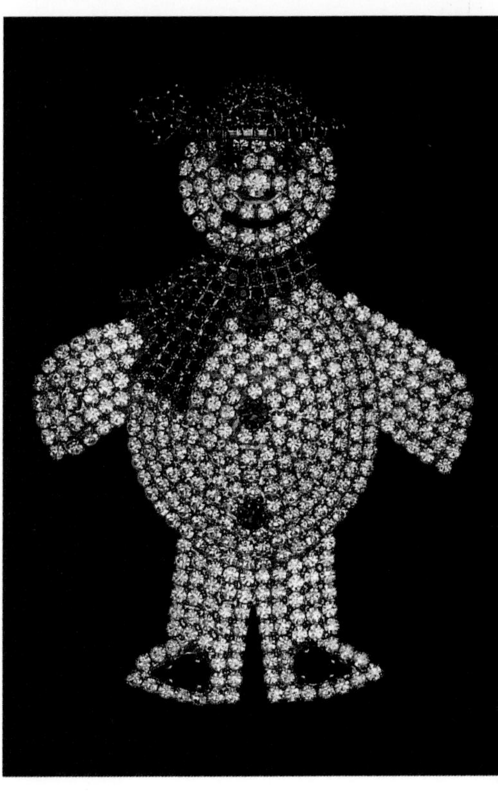

Fig 8.6 This unusual snowman by Butler and Wilson wears a broad-brimmed coal miner's hat with a lantern attached to the brim. His mouth is cut open to the back; he seems particularly white for a coal-mining snowman. 4.0" $175-225

Fig 8.7 a. A snow lady by Stephanie Sommers wears green and red holly on the front of her large, dark red baguette hat. As with other Stephanie Sommers pieces, her stones are glued directly to the back, without metal settings. 2.12" **b.** By Marvella, this snowman has a large faux pearl head and pearl-outlined body. He has one rhinestone at the knot of his gold bow and a jauntily placed gold stovepipe hat. 2.12" $15-30 each

Fig 8.8 a. A fanciful snowman by Don Lin—all enamel, no rhinestones. Made in three parts that are chain-linked, his hat rides so low that it covers his face. The broom in his left hand also hangs from a link. 3.12" **b.** Chain-link rhinestones cover this simple unsigned snowman. His neck scarf hangs loose. 3.0" $20-40 each

Fig 8.9 Three angels by MYLU. **a.** This angel floats along carrying the peace symbol. She has a red ribbon in her hair and two green eyes; the rest of the eighteen rhinestones decorate her dress. 2.25" **b.** A near-profile of this angel carrying a large red carnation. Her eyes are green rhinestones and she has tiny red stones embedded in her wings. 1.87" **c.** This angel sits face-forward under an oversized, red poinsettia. She has green eyes; there are six more green stones in the center of the poinsettia. 1.87" $15-35 each

Fig 8.10 a. The near-profile of an angel carrying a tiny Christmas tree. Tiny stones decorate her dress and the tree, and she has blue stone eyes—twenty-six stones in all. Signed *JJ.* 1.75" **b.** This angel is signed *DODDZ*. In profile, she appears to be flying straight ahead. She is gold with seventeen pale green stones in her dress. This piece was offered as a jewelry kit in 1968 by Jewel Creations. 1.75" $20-35 each

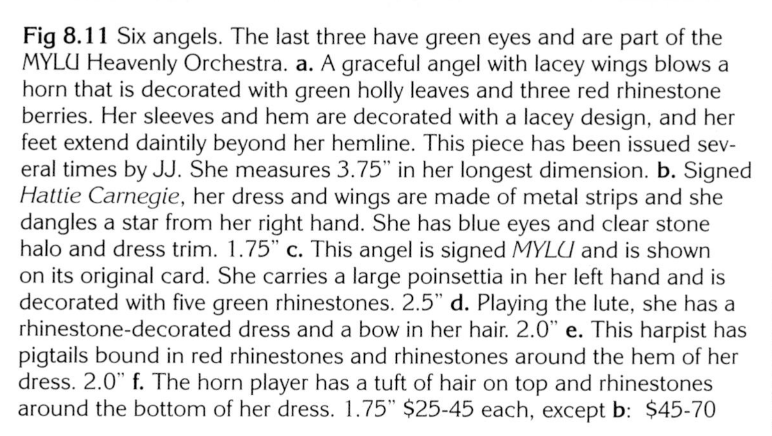

Fig 8.11 Six angels. The last three have green eyes and are part of the MYLU Heavenly Orchestra. **a.** A graceful angel with lacey wings blows a horn that is decorated with green holly leaves and three red rhinestone berries. Her sleeves and hem are decorated with a lacey design, and her feet extend daintily beyond her hemline. This piece has been issued several times by JJ. She measures 3.75" in her longest dimension. **b.** Signed *Hattie Carnegie*, her dress and wings are made of metal strips and she dangles a star from her right hand. She has blue eyes and clear stone halo and dress trim. 1.75" **c.** This angel is signed *MYLU* and is shown on its original card. She carries a large poinsettia in her left hand and is decorated with five green rhinestones. 2.5" **d.** Playing the lute, she has a rhinestone-decorated dress and a bow in her hair. 2.0" **e.** This harpist has pigtails bound in red rhinestones and rhinestones around the hem of her dress. 2.0" **f.** The horn player has a tuft of hair on top and rhinestones around the bottom of her dress. 1.75" $25-45 each, except **b**: $45-70

Fig 8.12 This Christmas elf by BJ holds a paint brush in his arm, which is hinged so it moves up and down. In his right hand he carries the alphabet block he has just finished painting. He walks above a *Merry Christmas* sign, and has two blue rhinestone eyes. 1.87" $10-30

Fig 8.13 a. With two batons and signed *MYLU*, this boy is either ready to conduct or twirl. He has two green rhinestone eyes. 2.0" **b.** A drummer boy signed *Corel*. He has holly on his tassel hat and no rhinestones. 2.0" $20-60 each

Chapter 9

Jewelry Care and Display

Proper storage of your Christmas jewelry collection will go a long way toward preventing problems. Your jewelry should be kept in a moisture- and dust-free environment, but tossing the pieces into a jewelry box where they might scratch one another is not a good solution. Nice costume jewelry can be kept in small plastic bags or, ideally, in boxes made for jewelry. When my collection was smaller, I bought cardboard boxes with glass tops to store pins. When my collection outgrew the box system, I was able to find the cabinet shown in Fig 9.1.

Most collectors agree that moisture is the principal cause of destruction to rhinestones. Moisture damage may not be apparent for some time because it collects between the stone and its foil backing, but it can eventually cause the stone to lose its luster and become dull. If you sometimes wear your pieces, remember to always apply any hair sprays or perfume *before* you put on your jewelry. These products can cause surface dulling on the jewelry.

Cleaning

If you have a piece of rhinestone jewelry that you feel needs cleaning, you might try some of the following ideas. Remember that too little cleaning is far better than too much—stop as soon as you feel you can live with the piece.

1. Gently brush the piece with a soft, clean brush (like a makeup brush) to remove dust from the crevices. (Aurora borealis stones are the exception to this advice. The coating on these stones scratches so readily that they shouldn't be brushed at all, unless you can cover the AB stone with a finger and brush around it. Otherwise, you should use the Q-Tip technique below.) Brushing may reveal loose stones, and you should reglue them now. Sometimes brushing is all that is needed. If so, stop here. If not, go to step 2.

2. Spray a bit of ammonia-based glass cleaner or denatured alcohol onto a very soft, worn-out toothbrush or piece of soft cotton material (like a T-shirt). Do *not* spray directly onto the jewelry. If using a brush, blot it repeatedly on a cloth. When you think there isn't any moisture left in the brush, run your thumb across it and watch for a mist. If it flips a mist into the air, it is still too wet. When the brush is sufficiently dry, brush the piece again. Once again, be careful of any aurora borealis stones, which will scratch.

Sometimes the cloth or a Q-Tip, squeezed dry, is easier and faster, and you won't have to worry as much about excess moisture. Whatever you use, it is best to dry the piece upside down, possibly on a cake rack or in front of a fan that will help speed evaporation.

Unless specific instructions to the contrary come with a brand new piece of jewelry, rhinestone jewelry should never be dunked in liquid!

Gluing

Sooner or later (usually, it is sooner), every jewelry collector comes to the point of having to replace stones. The most important thing about gluing is to use the right product. In almost every case, that will be a glue called Hypo-Tube Cement, sometimes referred to as "watch crystal glue." It will not turn yellow with age, and it is easy to apply—it comes in a tube with a long, narrow neck ideal for applications to tiny stone settings. If for some reason the rhinestone must be removed at a later date, that task will not be impossible if you use this glue.

Before setting a rhinestone in place, all the old glue and foil backing must be removed with a dental tool or other metal pick. The simplest method of inserting the stone is with a dop stick (waxed sticks for picking up stones). These are commercially available, but if you don't foresee doing this process over and over, you can make your own with a small ball of Stick Yack or Blu- Tack applied to the end of a toothpick. Use it to pick up the rhinestone by its upper face. Next, partly fill the setting with glue, being careful not to overfill it. Using your homemade dop stick, carefully lower the stone into the cup and level it with your thumb or finger.

Repairing

If you have more elaborate repairs, you can either consider taking or mailing your piece to a specialist. It is better to have the job done properly or not at all than to put in rhinestones of the wrong color, age, size, or shape. There are excellent costume jewelry repair experts in all parts of the country. Or, if you would like to tackle the job yourself, you can visit Janet Lawwill's website at http://www.SparklePlenty.com. She goes into more detail about the problems and possible solutions of repairing costume jewelry.

Fig 9.1 This is a turn-of-the-century (not the year 2000!) oak dental cabinet. Its many drawers make it possible to organize the pins into categories. The drawers are tall enough for pins, but would not be appropriate for wide bracelets or other jewelry. It keeps pins dust-free and easy to find.

Bibliography

Books

Ball, Joanne Dubbs. *Costume Jewelers, The Golden Age of Design.* Atglen, Pennsylvania, Schiffer Publishing Ltd, 1990.

Baker, Lillian. *100 Years of Collectible Jewelry.* Paducah, Kentucky, Collector Books, 1978.

Ettinger, Roseann. *Forties & Fifties Popular Jewelry.* Atglen, Pennsylvania, Schiffer Publishing Ltd, 1994.

———. *Popular Jewelry of the '60s, '70s & '80s.* Atglen, Pennsylvania, Schiffer Publishing Ltd, 1997.

Gallina, Jill. *Christmas Pins, Past and Present.* Paducah, Kentucky, Collector Books, 1996.

Simonds, Cherri. *Collectible Costume Jewelry*. Paducah, Kentucky, Collector Books, 1997.

Articles

Bailey, Laurel. "Christmas Present," *Vintage Fashion & Costume Jewelry Newsletter,* Fall, 1997.

Tempesta, Lucille. "Christmas Past and Present." *Vintage Fashion & Costume Jewelry Newsletter,* Fall, 1997.

Index of Signed Pieces